IS EUROPE CHRISTIAN?

Is Europe Christian?

OLIVIER ROY

Translated by
CYNTHIA SCHOCH

HURST & COMPANY, LONDON

First published in French by Editions du Seuil, January 2019, as
L'Europe est-elle chrétienne ?
This English language edition first published in the United
Kingdom in 2019 by
C. Hurst & Co. (Publishers) Ltd.,
41 Great Russell Street, London, WC1B 3PL
© Olivier Roy, 2019
English language translation © Cynthia Schoch, 2019

A Cataloguing-in-Publication data record for this book
is available from the British Library.

ISBN: 9781787381902

Printed and bound in Great Britain by Bell & Bain Ltd, Glasgow.

www.hurstpublishers.com

Contents

Introduction   1

1   Europe's Christian Heritage   7

2   Does Secularization Mean Dechristianization?   27

3   Another Source of Morality?   43
    The Church Versus Modernism (1864–1964)

4   The Self-Secularization of Religion   57

5   The Turning Point of the 1960s   71

6   The Religious Secession: 81
    The Encyclical *Humanæ vitæ* (July 1968)

7   Identity and Values: Europe and the Other   103

8   The End of Christian Europe or the End   125
    of Religion?

Conclusion   151

Notes   155

Index   171

Introduction

Three of the founding fathers of what is now the European Union—Robert Schuman of France, Alcide De Gasperi of Italy, and Konrad Adenauer of Germany—were devout Catholics. The first two are even shrouded in sanctity. To these men, it was obvious that Christianity was at the core of European identity, the soul at the centre of the huge bureaucratic body being constructed by politicians. And yet Christianity was never enshrined in the Treaty of Rome, which created the European Economic Community (EEC) in 1957. Perhaps it was considered better for Europe to be Christian not in letter but in spirit. Or maybe this pillar of European identity was so obvious that there was no need to carve it in stone.

The question arose fifty years later, in 2004, as the preamble was being written for the draft treaty for establishing a constitution for Europe. Backed by Pope Benedict XVI, some—mostly Catholics—urged that the document make mention of Europe's 'Christian roots'. Here it is worth mentioning that even to talk about 'roots' indicates a reluctance to state simply that 'Europe is Christian'. Moreover, if a reminder of such roots is deemed necessary in the text of a constitution, it is precisely because they cannot be taken for granted.

What exactly had happened in those fifty years? Since the Treaty of Rome, there have been two significant developments for Christianity in Europe. First, secularization has given way to the large-scale dechristianization of European societies in both religious and cultural terms, especially from the protests of 1968 onwards. Second, Islam has arrived in Europe, through immigration and, with Turkey's application for membership of the EU, the proposed expansion of the continent's borders. While populist movements since the 1990s have mainly mobilized against Islam, the Catholic Church has focused for much longer on the threat to Christian values represented by secularization, seen as a new form of paganism. In July 1968, Pope Paul VI issued the *Humanæ vitæ* papal encyclical condemning the erosion of traditional sexual morality and the tide of sexual liberation sweeping the West. John Paul II later doubled down on the Church's rejection of Europe's cultural secularization. He saw a return to faith as the solution, as he expressed in 1980 during a visit to France when he exclaimed, 'France, have you been faithful to the promises of your baptism?' According to John Paul II, the baptism of the first king of France, Clovis, enshrined

France's enduring loyalty to the Church; it was not a matter of mere cultural tradition. Later, when Benedict XVI campaigned for a reference to Europe's Christian roots, it was not Islam he had in mind. Rather, his concern was secular culture, which his predecessor had called a 'culture of death', and which he himself believed had led Christian Europe to convert to a new form of paganism in the space of a few decades.

In response to this encroachment, an entire Catholic revival movement was born, its primary aim being to fight the values of secularism. In France, for instance, La Manif Pour Tous (Demonstration for All) blamed same-sex marriage, and thus the collapse of the Christian West, on the new secular culture and its endorsement by complacent elites. Islam was not the main scapegoat; in fact, the movement made a huge effort to encourage Jews and Muslims to participate in its early marches. Naturally, Sens Commun, a political offshoot of La Manif Pour Tous, instantly made clear its hostility to immigration as well, yet the fact remains that the issues of abortion and same-sex marriage were more central to conservative Catholic mobilization. Meanwhile, Evangelical Protestants arrived on the scene of religious revivalism in the 1980s. They also vigorously criticized the dominance of cultural paganism, but without harking back to the Christian roots of Europe, which they do not consider the centre of the world. Evangelical Protestantism is uninterested in the past and nostalgia: the entire world is mission territory; globalization, the future.

Alongside the call of the churches, another movement also suddenly, but belatedly, began to remember Europe's Christian roots, though without preaching a return to faith—and for good reason, as its adherents can hardly be said to be religious. Populist movements and the conservative right, sometimes joined by left-leaning elements, champion Europe's 'Christian identity' in order to counter Islam. Such groups view this identity as a matter of culture rather than faith; few populists attend mass, and from the United Kingdom to France and Italy, the large majority of today's right are religiously indifferent. The Front National party platform for the 2017 presidential election in France did not even mention Christianity, and in fact planned to strengthen *laïcité* ('secularity'). Only one reference to churches can be found in its previous manifestos, with a promise in 2014 to ensure their preservation as historical monuments—a fine way of acknowledging their low attendance. When German interior minister Horst Seehofer declared, 'No, Islam is not part of Germany' in March 2018, he argued, 'Christianity has shaped Germany, including Sunday as a day of rest, church holidays, and rituals such as Easter, Pentecost and Christmas.'[1] Notably, his argument listed only cultural traits that have become totally secularized and unrelated to religious worship (what percentage of the European population sees Shrove Tuesday as anything more than an excuse to eat pancakes?). Most importantly, the 'European values' contrasted with the imagined ideals of newcomers are not Christian values—'love thy neighbour' has even been decried as self-flagellation by French public figures ranging from Jean-Marie Le Pen to philosopher Pascal Bruckner—but are instead the liberal values that came out of the Enlightenment and secularization, including freedom of conscience and criticism, sexual freedom, human rights and, more recently, gay rights. In other words, they are many of the very same values rejected or criticized by the Church (Pope Francis openly stated that he was 'not Charlie').

Of course, the followers of these two movements often overlap: La Manif Pour Tous activists readily vote for the Front National. Nevertheless, if we want to understand what is really going on, it is important to distinguish the diversity of perspectives.

The debate over Europe's Christian identity does not rest on a binary opposition between Europe and Islam, but on a triangle whose three poles are: 1) the Christian religion; 2) Europe's secular values (even if they occasionally make reference to a Christian identity); 3) Islam as a religion. The eternal question 'Is Islam compatible with democracy/ European values/secularism?' in fact raises another question: What do we set against Islam—is it Christianity or the Enlightenment? The question cannot be ingeniously sidestepped by claiming that secularism is the daughter of the Church or that the Church today has assimilated the message of the Enlightenment: with Benedict XVI, the Church undertook a critique of Enlightenment ideology, and many Catholic intellectuals, such as Rémi Brague, Pierre Manent, Marcello Pera and Ryszard Legutko, have followed in this vein.

But lurking behind the debate over Islam are much deeper questions about the very nature of Europe and its relationship to religion in general. The notion that Europe would be fine if only Islam or immigration did not exist is, of course, an illusion. There is a serious crisis surrounding European identity and the place of religion in the public sphere, as can be seen both in Christian radicalization over the issues of abortion and same-sex marriage, and in secular radicalization over religious slaughter and circumcision (behind Islam, the place of Judaism also comes into question). This is nothing short of a crisis in European culture.

1

Europe's Christian Heritage

The importance of Christianity in European history, even in the very idea of Europe, cannot be doubted. The area we call Europe today roughly corresponds to eleventh-century Latin Christendom, and it is self-evident that the main legal and political concepts that structured state-building, and later European integration, were forged in a Christian milieu.

A Christian Legacy?

It is well known that the first universities were religious institutions and that the first intellectuals were men of the clergy. Of course, this Christianity was not closed to the world: it benefitted from exchanges with and contributions from the Greeks, Romans, Muslims, Jews, and so on. The scholars of the time were receptive and took what they wanted where they could. But it would be a mistake to understand this philosophical open-mindedness, which was specific to the intellectual elite, as a feature of society as a whole, as, for instance, in the often imagined reconstruction of the Middle Ages, in which Al-Andalus is viewed as a model of religious coexistence. Such representations are, to a large extent, anachronistic constructions (what 'multiculturalism' was there to speak of in the Middle Ages?), exploited by the left and right alike to tackle contemporary issues. Ecumenical festivals of sacred music may be aesthetically satisfying, but they do not say much about relations between religious communities or theological debates of long ago. Even today, a culinary or musical repertoire can be shared without implying harmonious political coexistence—Palestinians and Israelis both enjoy falafel; Turks and Armenians both eat stuffed vine leaves. Conversely, if culture is taken in the anthropological sense, today's Europeans are very different from their medieval counterparts.[1] Nonetheless, history does have a role to play in explaining the present, in the development of philosophy, law and institutions, and in the construction of societies.

Incidentally, mention is often made today of a 'Judeo-Christian' Europe, but the expression is rather meaningless. If it aims to unite Judaism and Christianity by pointing at the latter's origins in the former, then it is not only redundant but also misguided, as Jews do not identify with what the Church has done with its Hebrew heritage. Moreover, to say that Judaism as such played a key role in the construction of European identity is a misunderstanding. What was passed on from Judaism to Christianity is what the Church allowed to pass, and it did not allow much. In 1239, for instance, Pope Gregory IX banned the Talmud, the key text and body of law in Jewish tradition. For the Church, one of the worst sins was to 'judaize' Catholicism; to be a 'Judeo-Christian' in sixteenth-century Spain could lead to being burned at the stake. The Church also determined who was ostracized in the ghetto and who could leave. When Jews were assimilated into the dominant culture in the nineteenth century, metaphorically and sometimes literally coming out of the ghetto, there was a boom in Yiddish culture, which, although influenced by religion, is largely secular and which developed primarily in Eastern Europe.

The Pope and the Emperor

The eleventh century is a key moment in Christianity's history: just when the Great Schism in 1054 brought about a permanent split between Latin Catholicism and Eastern Orthodoxy, the violent dispute between the pope and the emperor over the source of legitimacy and political power raised the question of the relationship between religion and politics, and between authority and power. The emperor, or rather the temporal sovereign, won out in the end, not through the victory of the secular over the religious, but through the redefinition of secular power as the expression of God's will. Power became legitimate per se as the reflection of God's will, and power prevails over knowledge. This theological–political matrix would play a key role in the development of the concept of the sovereign nation and, within that, of the Law as the expression of political will, and not of natural law. All this was extensively developed and debated during the Middle Ages in a de facto European arena, where clergymen all wrote in Latin and circulated and shared ideas independently of their 'national' affiliation. Early on, the Church offered a 'supranationality' (if this anachronism can be allowed, the concept of the nation-state having been constructed gradually over centuries).

Beyond this political theology of sovereignty limited by natural law, which would easily become secularized, Christianity had a fundamental impact in other areas of life. The twin phenomena of the Inquisition and the sacrament of penance, or confession, led to the concept of one's 'heart of hearts' or innermost being centred, as Foucault showed in his later work, around the questions of truth and self, which would become core notions in psychoanalysis (a profoundly 'Catholic' science, as Lacan always said). Such highly specialized activities as police investigations (gathering evidence, questioning neighbours and extracting a confession, the latter still constituting a major part of police work in Catholic Europe) and criminal trials (where the defendant's truth comes out in his or her speech) were designed by Church jurists and by the Inquisition in particular. The Council of Trent played an important role in the elaboration of a Christian anthropological model that continues to hold sway across Europe: the family is nuclear, organized around man and wife and not the group, and there is symmetry between spouses, which is indeed a break from the Roman law perspective. In this regard, the anthropological structure of Western European societies (and not only law and politics) can be said to have been deeply influenced by Christianity. Naturally, we are talking about Latin Christianity, which, in its obsession with having the sin named and thereby recognized by the sinner, moved away from the Eastern version, which was more concerned with the glory of God than with man's wretchedness.

The Protestant Reform

The second key moment came at the turn of the sixteenth century with the discovery of the New World and, in 1517, the publication of Martin Luther's *95 Theses*. These events— the colonization of the Americas and the Protestant Reformation—radically altered Europe's view of itself. With these events began a long period of turmoil that ended in 1648 with the treaties of Westphalia, which established a new order based on state territorial sovereignty and gave states control over religion. No longer was any religious body above the state. This situation prompted the Church to gradually establish its autonomy; it became separate from the states of Europe and in so doing became a global force.

The Reformation ushered in a new religious culture. From that moment on, it makes little sense to speak of Christian Europe; it is more appropriate to refer instead to

Protestant Europe or Catholic Europe. Now we need to ask what remains common to both and what pertains to two different religious cultures. Moreover, we need to ask if it makes sense to talk about 'Protestant culture' in general; not only is the Lutheran tradition very different from Calvinism, but also, more importantly, the emergence of the United States as the embodiment of a new model of globalization after the First World War brought about a confusion between Americanization and Protestantization, even though the forms of American Protestantism have hardly dominated in Europe.

But, aside from differences in religiosity, it is obvious that the divide between a Protestant Europe and a Catholic Europe profoundly altered the cultural landscape. It can be found today in details that are as essential as they are trivial, from suicide rates to household savings and the furnishing of hotel rooms (twin beds in Protestant countries, 'matrimonial' [double] beds in Catholic countries: a little-known requirement of the Council of Trent). If the border between Flemish Belgium and the Netherlands, first and foremost a religious border, is anything to go by, it must be acknowledged that food is better in Catholic lands (Irish 'cuisine' still bears the deplorable effects of British imperialism today).

Yet, it would be very dangerous to essentialize this divide. Many clichés do not hold up in the long run: there is no real difference between Catholic fertility rates and Protestant fertility rates; Catholic capitalism does not pale in comparison to its Protestant rival, even if the latter has more robust theological backing, according to Max Weber; populism is alive and well in both the North and the South, even if Protestant populism is more socially progressive than its Catholic counterpart. Even if the only Swiss cantons that voted against banning minarets in 2009 were Protestant, the populist base is nevertheless strongest in historically Protestant cantons. The Confessing Church in Germany, which took a stand against Nazism, may well have been Protestant, but it was in Protestant Prussia and not Catholic Bavaria that the Nazi party achieved its highest scores. To see in Anglo-Saxon Protestantism the epitome of the culture of globalization is to ignore its history and complexity, particularly given the profound divide between Lutheranism and Calvinism, and the mutations of Calvinism in the Americas. There is a big difference between the self-secularization specific to Lutheranism and the resurgence of Evangelical Calvinism in the United States. Anglo-Saxon common law, which is moving to replace Roman-based law in European institutions (for instance in the Court of Human Rights in Strasbourg), is a product not of Protestantism but of Middle Age monasteries under the French-speaking and Catholic Plantagenet dynasty.

But what matters to us here is less the differences in religious culture than the political consequence of the Wars of Religion, that is, the establishment of the Westphalian state. As 'religious peace' proved to be an unattainable goal, politics ended up determining the place of religion in Europe. And this scenario still prevails.

The Wars of Religion and the Westphalian State: 1517–1648

Europe's great trauma dates back to the Wars of Religion between Catholics and Protestants, from the start of the Reformation until the Peace of Westphalia. The conflicts began with theological questions—about grace and salvation—considered by the actors to be essential and non-negotiable. The last two of Martin Luther's 95 *Theses* left no room for compromise: 'Christians should be exhorted to be diligent in following Christ, their Head, through penalties, death and Hell. And thus be confident of entering into Heaven through many tribulations rather than through the false security of peace (Acts 14:22).'

The Impossibility of a Religious Peace Settlement

It is, of course, possible to argue that the Reformation was more an expression of, rather than a trigger for, upheaval in the social, cultural and intellectual frameworks of the time, which had brought new actors to the fore. The fact nevertheless remains that people killed each other over matters of dogma and faith. Violence is religious in both its substance and its execution, as scholars such as Olivier Christin and Denis Crouzet have shown. Religion does not allow for negotiation, despite the ceaseless efforts of kings and emperors (such as François I and Charles V) to persuade theologians in both camps to reach a compromise; the colloquies of Poissy (1561), Worms (1557) and Regensburg (1541–46) all failed. Religious groups then proved themselves incapable of making peace through negotiation, because only the place of religion, and not religious dogma, can be negotiated (let that be a warning to French secularists[2] who seek to reform Islam). Interfaith dialogue continues to be promoted today as a means of preventing religious violence, but it does not work any better now than it did in the sixteenth century. Religious conflicts cannot be resolved by theological debate. Taking theology as a starting point leads to an impasse.

Political actors in the sixteenth and seventeenth centuries gradually realized that the Wars of Religion could not be won. The most interesting case here is that of Charles V, Holy Roman Emperor. Charles was a devout Catholic and a slayer of Protestant heretics. He was obsessed by the apocalypse, and dreamed of unifying Christendom, in other words Europe, against the Turks. Profoundly European himself (his mother tongue was French, and the Spanish demanded, probably in vain, that he learn Castilian to rule in Madrid; he did not speak German either when he arrived in Germany in 1521 to try to set Luther straight), he was the first to sign a 'religious peace'—the Peace of Augsburg in 1555—which recognized the right of rulers to choose the religion of their state.[3] Ironically, it was his own troops, Lutheran *Landsknechte*, as iconoclastic as they were thuggish, who perpetrated the tragic sack of Rome in 1527.

As Christin has shown, it was now politics that decided the place of religion.[4] The state ended up establishing 'religious peace' itself by determining the place of religion and thus resolving the age-old conflict between the pope and the emperor, to the latter's advantage. This is the meaning of the principle *Cuius regio, eius religio* ('whose realm, his religion'): the sovereign decides on religion. The state set the rules of the game, and this remains true today. The modern nation-state was formed in 1648 following the treaties of Westphalia, in which territorial sovereignty was a central principle of the political order. The Westphalian state is secular, but it is not anti-religious; indeed, the state controls the religious sphere. This is a consequence of the sea change that the Reformation introduced in Europe by breaking up the universal influence of the Catholic Church. From then on, people were no longer Christian but were Catholic or Protestant. Moreover, political authority came to manage the distribution and balance of power.

The success of the Reformation put an end to the Church's claim over political life. The Catholic Church would later reassert its claim to universality via globalization, but it was no longer the 'soul' of political Europe. However, this was not a period of separation of church and state, and politics still intervened directly in the realm of religion. The 1682 Declaration of the French Clergy, for instance, initiated by Louis XIV of France, asserted the supremacy of the ecumenical councils over the pope. Nor did the Reformation hail the advent of religious freedom, or even tolerance. These would come later, with the Edict of Toleration for Protestants in France in 1787; the Catholic emancipation in the UK, culminating in the Roman Catholic Relief Act of 1829; and as late as 1967 for Spanish Protestants and Jews. The first explicit affirmation of freedom of religion would not occur until the famous First Amendment to the United States Constitution in 1791.

In Europe, secularization has accompanied the genealogy of the nation-state, but, at the same time, the continent's culture remains Christian. The new state did not just control religious institutions. In its Lutheran version, which has been widely exported, the state appropriated religious moral norms and secularized them through profane legislation. The Lutheran state also assumed a certain number of the Church's functions (after confiscating its wealth), in particular in the realms of charity and education. Hospices and hospitals in Protestant areas come under the state, as the Church disappeared as an autonomous economic power. In other places, while the Church has retained a major role, it can no longer replace or compete with the state.

During this time, another critical prerogative fell away from the Church into the hands of the state: it had now become incumbent upon the state to promote virtue and concern itself with defining social morality. The state was no longer merely the secular arm of spiritual authority, it now had to take charge of the question of good and evil. And so appeared the offence of blasphemy and laws concerning morals, on 'debauchery', prostitution, adultery and abortion.[5] The state began to lock up deviants, the judge replaced the priest, and the law rendered private confession pointless. Sin was transmuted into crime. The state has even been known to criminalize matters that the Church allowed, such as begging and prostitution. 'Virtue' became a political value—the French Revolution would use the word to excess. Still, we remained in the same framework of good and evil. Irreligion was considered a great social ill and a breach of public order (Robespierre gave a speech before the National Convention denouncing atheism).[6] With regard to the extension of the new state model, it is therefore incorrect to speak of liberalism or dechristianization; more accurately, these centuries brought about the secularization of religious norms, in both their definition and their enforcement. That is also why we can still talk about 'Christian culture'.

Religion and the Modern State

A general conclusion can be drawn from the Wars of Religion. Ultimately, it is always the state that determines the place of religion in society, and so in this regard, all states are secular. However, that has no bearing on their populations' religiosity. There are secular states in which religious practice is strong, for instance, the United States, where the First Amendment provides a basis for the separation of religion and politics. While in France this separation protects politics from religion, in the US system it protects religion from politics. The United States nevertheless remains a country where strict separation of church and state prevails. The American paradox is that religious practice was lower when states financed the clergy, and the great wave of religious 'awakenings' in the early nineteenth century that forged the American religious mentality accompanied the effective implementation of the distance between church and state.[7] In France, the Law of 1905 first separated the Catholic Church from the republican state. This separation was extended to all religions, but it did not have the same impact on non-Catholics, as Jews and Protestants were in favour of the law. Another example is reunified Italy, which was boycotted by the Catholic Church. In the *Non expedit* pontifical decree in 1868, the Church separated itself from the new Italian state, even when the large majority of the country's population continued to be both very religious and patriotic.

Empires dealt better with religious diversity because they could accept the existence of differentiated spaces, whether horizontal (the periphery had greater freedom) or vertical (one had a choice of which transcendent power to appeal to). The nation-state, on the other hand, has the problem of the homogeneity of its territorial space and its relationship to transcendence. It is true that there are 'federal' republics, but federalism should not be mistaken for diversity; in fact, federalism always occurs where there is some homogeneity, such as in the United States, where individual states that have never been delimited by linguistic, ethnic or cultural differences agree to delegate a share of their power to a central government they have chosen.[8]

Even in states that claim to be religious, such as the Islamic Republic of Iran, politics also defines the religious sphere. Nowhere is there an autonomous and independent religious authority that can dictate to the state what a religious state should be. For example, although the Iranian constitution set up the Guardian Council to verify the compliance of parliamentary legislation with Islamic law, conflict between the two institutions was incessant, which led to the establishment of a third body, the Assembly of Experts. This body is supposed to bring the Guardian Council and the parliament to agreement. It is made up of men in government, leaders who took part in the revolution, and is essentially political.

Nowhere would a theologian call on a dictator, president or any executive power to dispute a political decision in religious terms, at least not with impunity. Such a person would invariably wind up in prison, as happens in Iran and Saudi Arabia (and once upon a time at the stake, like Savonarola in Florence). Regarding this theocratic optical illusion, Saudi Arabia is also a case in point. The monarchy claimed not to need a constitution because the Qur'an is its constitution and *sharia* its law. And then one fine day in 2017, the crown prince shattered this illusion by bringing the clergy to heel without anyone batting an eyelid, as everyone knew where the real power lay.[9]

The Globalization of Christianity

Following the Age of Discovery and the first phase of colonial expansion, Europe no longer had a monopoly on Christianity. At the very start of the sixteenth century, the Catholic Church quickly undertook a worldwide missionary project.[10] Overseas, it again encountered the problem of tension with European states, but this time in their colonial guise. The colonizing states (Portugal, Spain, and later France) wanted to take control of the Catholic Church in their newly acquired territory. This was the principle of *padroado* ('patronage' in Portuguese), recognized by Pope Paul III in the bull *Aequum reputamus* (1534): the colonial power could oversee the appointment of bishops; it financed the clergy and the construction of churches; and, above all, it had the monopoly on control of the missions. In effect, this meant that the colonial churches were mere subsidiaries of the metropole. Thus the Portuguese would forbid sending non-Portuguese missionaries to India, Spain reserved the right to control missions in the Americas, and Colbert gave the French Holy Orders the monopoly on the evangelization of 'New France' in North America.

But while recognizing the principle of *padroado*, the Church constantly circumvented it by establishing new missionary orders, the most significant being the Society of Jesus, or the Jesuits, approved in 1540 by the same Paul III, as well as new institutions such as the Sacred Congregation for the Propagation of the Faith, founded in 1599, which answered directly to Rome and recruited missionaries from all countries and assigned them missionary territory regardless of their nationality of origin. To get around the 'colonial' bishops, who were nationals of, and chosen by, their metropole, Rome appointed 'vicars apostolic' who answered solely to the Holy See and were recruited irrespective of nationality. The Church also took charge of training an indigenous clergy (in the mid-sixteenth century for Mexico, a century later for China). In 1658, Pope Alexander VII approved the establishment of the Society of Foreign Missions, a missionary institution that was independent of colonial parent states. The Church thus organized a 'globalized Catholicism'.

This naturally created tensions with the colonizing states. The Society of Jesus became a thorn in their side. The autonomous Jesuit missions in Paraguay (where the official language was Guarani) were destroyed by the Portuguese in 1767 and the Jesuits expelled. During the same period, the Society was banned in European countries, which refused the growing influence of a deterritorialized religious order (one that might today be described as 'cosmopolitan') that answered only to Rome. Successive expulsions would follow from 1763 to 1880, including in 1847 in the tolerant Swiss Confederation. Unable to impose itself as the suzerain, at least in spiritual terms, of European sovereigns, the Church developed a 'worldwide spiritual government'.

The nineteenth century was also a period of tension between the Church and European governments, as political anticlericalism mounted. This tension fostered the development of what in France was called ultramontanism, meaning believers' allegiance and direct loyalty to the pope, to the detriment of all forms of Gallicanism and of advocates of national or conciliar churches. The first Vatican Council (1870) asserted papal infallibility, ratifying the pope's absolute control over the Church at a time when he was losing what remained of the papal states. The missionary movement provided the Vatican with a remarkable instrument with which to wield influence worldwide. In short, never had the Church been as strong, and never had the papacy had as much control of the Church, as in the century when it lost the political battle in Europe. The crisis peaked with the mobilization to protect the pope during the Capture of Rome in 1870: the first 'international brigade' in European history was the battalion of Papal Zouaves that came to defend Rome in vain against the Italian army.

Christianity as it was preached in the missions was entirely European, and the seminary curriculum for the native populations in colonized countries was the same as in

Europe. In this regard, the Church engaged in stripping the colonized peoples of their identity and westernizing them. At the same time, missionaries used local languages and often introduced a writing system. Many had a distant relationship with the secular colonial powers and trained indigenous elites who would later be involved in independence movements. And finally, a significant proportion of missionaries would develop the theory of inculturation (which would not be named as such until the mid-twentieth century, but would be practised by certain Jesuits in China as early as the sixteenth century): it involved adopting the indigenous culture and transforming it from within through the message of the scriptures.

Not only did this 'indigenous' Christianity take root, but it gained a majority in the colonies, helping to pave the way for independence. In short, the ties between Europe and Christianity slackened. For a long time, missionaries were white and European. Today that is no longer the case, and the opposite is even true:[11] in the twenty-first century, churches in the Global South have turned things around. Catholic parishes in Europe are witnessing the arrival of African priests, and working-class suburbs are seeing the arrival of evangelical missionaries from the South. The third-worldization of Christian churches is, of course, a result of broad demographic trends, but more than that, it also corresponds to a religious revivalism and a wave of conversions or adherence to Charismatic movements that is much stronger in the South than in Europe. This Christianity that has come (back) from the South is far more conservative than the dominant version in Europe. The idol of Catholic traditionalists in France is the Guinean cardinal Robert Sarah, the model of the good clergyman who resists modernism.[12] This affects all Christian denominations: Anglican bishops in Kenya, Uganda and Nigeria all reject the ordination of homosexuals, and the new evangelical pastors operating in Europe reject the liberalism that has dominated European Protestantism since the nineteenth century. The election of the first non-European pope, Francis, in 2013, is evidence of the shift in Catholicism's centre of gravity away from Europe.

Protestantism has also experienced a similar shift away from old Europe, but in two stages. Starting in the early nineteenth century, it was the United States of America that became the centre of the missionary movement, all the more global as it was not tethered to a project of territorial colonization, as was the case for Anglicanism. From the Middle East to China, American missions were the most active up until the 1950s. Then, starting in the second half of the twentieth century, a form of revivalism developed, as had happened with Catholicism, that found a springboard in the countries of the South, in particular in Latin America and South Korea (the country that supplies the most Protestant missionaries in the world in terms of percentage of its population).

The globalization of Christianity has inherently altered its relationship to Europe. Even if Europe continues to perceive itself as Christian, Christianity is only marginally European. The globalization of Christianity has nevertheless not eroded the notion that Europe is Christian, because globalization in this case is seen as the westernization of the world due to colonialism. Yet such a viewpoint disregards two phenomena: inculturation, in other words, the appropriation of various forms of Christianity by local actors (evident, for instance, in Latin America and Africa); and the new nature of globalization, which is less the exportation of a Western cultural model than it is the deculturation of traditional modes of belief and communication, including in Europe. In both cases, we have moved very quickly from a primarily Italian Catholic Church, to the same Church in its European version, to end up today with a Church centred on the non-European world, in other words, to the southward shift of Christianity. While Popes John Paul II and Benedict XVI were obsessed with the question of European culture, it does not seem a central preoccupation for Pope Francis.

Europe is thus no longer at the heart of Christianity. But is Christianity still at the heart of Europe?

2

Does Secularization Mean
Dechristianization?

In what sense has Europe remained Christian since the Peace of Westphalia in 1648? Of course, from then on, there has no longer been only one form of Christianity: a choice has to be made between Protestantism and Catholicism. But more important is the development, from the eighteenth century onward, of what is commonly called secularization. The term actually refers to two different phenomena, which may or may not coincide.

The Two Types of Secularization

The first form of secularization is based on a legal and constitutional concept: the autonomy of the political sphere, leading either to the separation of the state from religious institutions (as in France and the United States), or to the political takeover of the religious sphere. Examples in history include Gallicanism in the Kingdom of France and Josephinism under the Habsburg Monarchy, while today we might add the churches in Scandinavia, as well as states where a concordat is in force, where some religions or churches have official status, but in a framework defined and limited by the public authorities (such as in Belgium and Germany). This hegemony of the political is called *laïcité* in France, even if the word does not figure in the Law of 1905, which separated the church and state, and even if it took on a more ideological than legal connotation during the twentieth century.[1]

The second form of secularization is sociological in nature: it denotes the decline in religious observance and the disappearance of religion as the focus of social and cultural life. This is what is called dechristianization in Europe.

But again, the two forms of secularization are not necessarily concomitant. There can be separation between the church and state in countries whose society remains deeply religious (Italy after the unification of 1871, the United States). Historically speaking, Louis XIV, a champion of Gallicanism, was a devout Catholic, as was General de Gaulle, but both were committed to putting the Church in its place. Conversely, largely dechristianized countries can have a state church (Scandinavian countries, England). The two forms of 'secularism' go together in France; this is a specific feature of French *laïcité*, as in France not only is religion separate from the state, but radical secularists also campaign to limit its visibility in the public sphere.

Secularization therefore does not necessarily mean dechristianization, but in Europe they happen to go together and dechristianization is measurable in sociological terms. There has been an abundance of reputable research since the 1950s demonstrating the decline in religious practice and vocations in Christian Europe. This research will not be reviewed in detail, but instead I will give a few concrete examples. First, it should be remembered that the main question addressed here is not the fact of dechristianization, which has been studied extensively by others, but its relationship to culture: does the decline in practice go together with a mere secularization of values, which remain basically Christian in their content, or does Europe define itself today according to references and values that churches no longer recognize as Christian?

For instance, historians have studied wills written in the seventeenth and eighteenth centuries, looking at the number of requests to have a funeral mass, and donations left to religious institutions to secure the salvation of one's soul.[2] The decline is very obvious, at least among men. In the nineteenth century, dechristianization was masked by the rise in gendered differences in relation to the Catholic Church: women still went to church, but men no longer accompanied them. While the clergy remained male, parish attendance became increasingly female, and the number of women exceeded the number of men in religious orders. In addition to research by historians,[3] twentieth-century sociologists of religion established objective criteria for measuring religious practice among Catholics.[4] As regards the Catholic Church, their work was greatly facilitated by the fact that the Church is also a huge bureaucracy that keeps registers of mass attendance, donations, annual numbers of baptisms, confessions, marriages, and so on. Even today, the Church keeps a register of conversions: we know, for example, just how many Muslims convert to Catholicism each year. Statistics on Protestant religious practice are less rigorous and less centralized, and for Muslims there are none.

The two forms of secularization—political and legal secularization (the separation of church and state or control of the church by the state) on one hand and sociological secularization (the decline in religious practice) on the other—may not seem spatially and temporally synchronized, but in Europe they ended up coinciding. Secularization has been a long-term and steady process, albeit punctuated by sudden breaks that vary by country. When the treaties of Westphalia were signed in 1648, marking the beginning of political secularization, all of Europe was religious. In France, the long process of dechristianization began in the eighteenth century: the old Catholic lands of Île-de-France, where the Catholic League put up resistance to the future King Henri IV, collapsed, and from 1876 to 1914 the population voted systematically for the anticlerical republicans. There followed a slow decline in religious practice, and then a sharp drop in the mid-1960s. In France, regular mass-attending Catholics made up a mere 4.5 per cent of the French population in 2010, compared to 27 per cent in 1952.[5]

At the other end of the spectrum is Ireland, where the drop in religiosity was not preceded by a long decline, because the Church retained a dominant position owing to the link between nationalism and Catholicism (even if the founders of the Irish national movement in the nineteenth century were Protestant) up until around the 1990s. The continuity was broken by a very sudden dechristianization at the turn of the twenty-first century: whereas in 1983 the ban on abortion was passed by 67 per cent voting in favour in a referendum, in 1995, a pivotal year, legalization of divorce was approved by 50.3 per cent of the vote. Then, in 2015, same-sex marriage was ratified by 62.07 per cent of the vote, and legalization of abortion in May 2018 by 68 per cent. A complete turnaround in the space of a single generation!

Somewhere between these two countries is Spain, a Catholic land if ever there was one, where only 109 priests were ordained in 2017 and the number of self-declared Catholics is equal to France.[6] The principle of same-sex marriage was passed when the left was in power in 2004, but the right did not overturn it when it came back into office in 2011, evidence of a phenomenon that will be returned to later: nearly everywhere in Europe, the right has ceased to be the champion of Christian values and Church rights in the face of a supposedly secular left.

In Protestant countries, the decline in religious practice has been steady: in the United Kingdom, 48.6 per cent of the population declared they had no religion in 2015, 43 per cent identified as Christians and 8.4 per cent said they were affiliated with a religion other than Christianity.[7] In all European countries there is a clear gap between those who identify as Christian (who are a majority, whether absolute or relative) and those who truly believe in religious teachings, the latter tending to drop below 10 per cent.

The Second Vatican Council: The Beginning of the End?

It is essential to date dechristianization if we want to understand its causes. In France and Quebec, it began around 1965; the plunge occurred brutally, in the space of some ten years, that is, in less than a generation. In other words, the drop in practice affected people who still practised and who suddenly ceased to do so (whereas in Ireland it seems more connected with the arrival of a new generation). This suddenness prompted Guillaume Cuchet to conclude that it was a consequence of the Second Vatican Council, or Vatican II, which took place in four sessions from 1962 to 1965 and set out to reconsider the Catholic Church's relationship with the modern world.[8] But, aside from the fact that is hard to imagine that an event as complex as Vatican II could have an immediate impact on well-entrenched religious practices, harbingers of such a drop obviously predate the Council. The decline in priestly vocations in France began suddenly after the year 1948 (when there was a spike of 2,000 ordinations), stabilizing at fewer than 100 ordinations as of 2000. There is no correlation with the date of the Council. A slight increase was even noted in the two years following the Council.[9]

Dechristianization is associated with deep sociological trends already underway prior to the Council, such as urbanization and the disappearance of the peasantry, illustrated by Henri Mendras' book *La Fin des paysans*,[10] published in 1967, whose research dates back to the decade preceding the Council. The dechristianization of the working class began even earlier, but awareness of it came late, with a decisive turning point in 1942, at the time when Abbé Henri Godin's book *France, pays de mission?* was published, calling for a new missionary movement in response to dechristianization. Dechristianization did not occur uniformly across social classes and regions, and so cannot simply be put down to an urban/rural division. But in any case, the watershed marked by the 1960s largely evened out the phenomenon, despite the fact that the regional variable still seemed quite prevalent in the early 1960s.

In other European countries, the turning point towards dechristianization has occurred at different times, and thus did not directly correlate with Vatican II. As in France, the phenomenon elsewhere in Europe affected all social categories. In Ireland, however, the impact of Vatican II was not immediately felt: the percentage of weekly churchgoers in 1974 was still 91 per cent. But it plunged to 64 per cent in 1995.[11] Given that the most religious are found among older age groups, the drop in religiosity was certainly stronger among under 50s. The 2018 abortion referendum seems to indicate a relative levelling out between urban and rural areas and between generations: all social and age groups voted 'yes', although in different proportions.

As for the correlation between scandals and decline in religious practice, paedophilia in the Church has often been mentioned as a reason for the latter. At the same time, it is precisely because the Church is no longer untouchable that it can be criticized, and its misdeeds discussed. Shocking episodes such as the Magdalene laundries, penitentiary workhouses for 'fallen women' in Ireland, preceded the Council, but the code of silence was not lifted until much later. The last Magdalene laundry was closed in 1996, at about the same time as scandals about paedophilia among priests were erupting. The case of Ireland provides another interesting correlation, this time between the Northern Ireland peace process and the decline in religious practice, which accelerated just after the Good Friday Agreement in 1998. This could be said to illustrate the deconfessionalization of nationalism. A similar phenomenon occurred in Quebec: Quebecois nationalism and the Front de libération du Québec emerged when the power of the Church had dissipated. The same connection can also be found in 1970s' Brittany.[12]

These evolutions illustrate the relative nature of the association between religion and nationalism. The two most striking cases, aside from Ireland, are the Czech Republic and Poland. In Poland, Catholicism has always been tied to national identity, as opposed to Russian Orthodoxy to the east and Prussian Lutheranism to the west. In the Czech Republic, it is the opposite: Catholicism stood against nationalist aspirations. Bohemia was massively won over to Protestantism in the sixteenth century, and it was the Habsburg reconquest that imposed Catholicism after the Battle of the White Mountain in 1620. Catholicism therefore never really took hold, except in architecture. Secularization can also be said to be the expression of peaceful nationalism in Bohemia. In any case, there is no sign of a religious revival in the Czech Republic, and certainly no more so than in countries where nationalism and Catholicism are linked. In Poland, although the number of priests rose after the fall of communism, the number of seminarians has halved since peaking in the year 2000, and the number of *dominicantes*, parishioners who attend mass regularly, fell from 57 per cent in 1982 (at the height of the papacy of John Paul II, a Pole) to 36 per cent in 2016.[13] In short, there has been a ratchet effect: dechristianization never takes a step backward.

The link between Catholicism and nationalism may enable religion to endure for a while, but it in no way guarantees continuity in the long term (as Quebec and Ireland attest). This is even clearer for Protestantism (in

Scandinavia and the UK, as well as Northern Ireland for unionists). While such associations may reinforce nationalism, they also secularize the religious. As will be seen later, they in fact tend to reduce religion to a mere question of identity. The electoral victory of the Catholic populist Law and Justice (PiS) party in Poland may thus paradoxically lead to a breach between identity and faith. After all, identity is not the custodian of faith.

When Christian Identity No Longer Means Faith in Christ

The correlation between Vatican II and the sharp drop in religious vocations is thus not necessarily one of causality between the former and the latter. One can just as easily argue that the new Church lost its appeal and magic, and thus was deserted by its followers, or that the Council took place because the clergy was aware of a drop in practice and had to come up with something else to bring worshippers back. In any case, it is obvious that the Council was only possible because of dechristianization, either as a consequence or an active cause among others. Vatican II was also meant to address secularization, taking it into account for the first time. It came to be viewed as a new sort of value, which, as we shall see, led to a sort of self-secularization or at least desacralization.

In any event, barring a few exceptions, the number of regularly practising Christians in most countries in Western

Europe has tended to drop below the 10 per cent mark in the twenty-first century. The decline in practice is particularly high among young people, which bodes ill for a 'religious comeback' (this expression will be discussed in detail later). It is true that significant percentage of Europeans continue to identify as Christians,[14] but it would be a mistake to view them as 'occasionally practising' Christians. In fact, they no longer practise their religion at all, even if they go to weddings and funerals. Many identify as Christians while rejecting the Church's essential dogmas, from Mary's virginity to the very existence of God. In a 2007 poll, 59 per cent of French people identified as Catholics, but only 15 per cent of them said they attended mass at least once a month, which brings the percentage of practising Catholics to less than 10 per cent of the entire French population. Moreover, only 38 per cent of the French claim to believe in 'some sort of God' (which thus includes among the non-believers a large portion of those who identify as Catholics). Moreover, 73 per cent of the 25–34 age group say that religion is not important in their life.[15] While 76 per cent of Danes say they belong to the Lutheran Church, only 25 per cent say they believe that Jesus is the son of God and 8 per cent accept Mary's virginity, young people being even more sceptical than their elders.[16]

This discrepancy in surveys between those who identify as Christian, those who state they are believers and those who practise is also found in countries with a strong Catholic tradition. According to a study in 2015 by the Centro de Investigaciones Sociológicas, only 13.7 per cent of Spanish people go to mass, amounting to barely 10 per cent of the 75 per cent who identify as Catholic.[17] The figure is the same in Germany, where the percentage of regularly practising Christians went from 18.6 per cent in 1995 to 10.4 per cent in 2015.[18]

The trouble with these polls is that they use the same categories as Gabriel Le Bras and Canon Boulard, which suppose a continuity between regularly practising Christians and other Christians, which made sense prior to the 1960s. It is clear that today, non-practising people who identify as Christians no longer even occasionally practise the essential rites of the Church, such as confession and communion once a year, which was a measurement criteria of 'occasional Christians' in Canon Boulard's surveys. Rather, they only attend mass for reasons of sociability, conformism, and even festivity—at weddings and funerals—where they are consumers more than worshippers.[19] At the same time, they tick the 'Christian' (or 'Catholic' or 'Protestant') box in surveys. These are Europeans for whom Christianity is an identity reference, and not at all a religious reference.

One can of course identify with Christian culture and not believe in God, like the right-wing French politician Charles Maurras in the early twentieth century, or even Jean-Marie Le Pen, for whom faith matters little. Even so,

Catholicism in particular plays a fundamental role in Europe, because the continent's dominant culture is considered a secularized version of Christianity. This purely identitarian reference has probably been reinforced by the rise of Islam in Europe. In any case, it has been taken up by populist movements and the conservative right, without apparently prompting any kind of revival of religious practice. The crux of the matter is thus to know what this reference to Christianity equates to. Is it a 'cold', secularized religion, or purely an identity marker referring to a value system that no longer has anything Christian about it?

Has Christian Identity Survived the End of Faith?

The decline in religious practice across Europe does not necessarily make references to religious identity irrelevant. If, as Marcel Gauchet famously wrote, Christianity is 'the religion for departing from religion', then the dominant European culture is a form of secularized Christianity. This thesis has existed in various forms since Feuerbach, and even Hegel, and was taken up by Max Weber and Pierre Legendre. That people no longer believe in God does not mean society is no longer Christian in its values, such as respect for human dignity, and its institutions. One can also point to the Christian influence on law, or the role of the Inquisition in shaping the conduct of police investigations and the importance of confession. The artistic and philosophical cultures of modern Europe are also well grounded in Christianity. Descartes himself spent a lot of time trying to prove the existence of God in order to make up for his *cogito* that rendered God unnecessary.

It is thus possible to defend the idea of Europe's Christian identity and assert its 'Christian roots' without denying the drop in practice and the disappearance of faith. But is Christian heritage enough to say that Europe today is still culturally Christian? Religion is not, in and of itself, a mould or producer of culture. It is an operator that must constantly explain itself, prove its truth, demonstrate that it is not simply culture, in other words profane, either via the asceticism of a philosophy aiming for transcendence, or by the constraints it imposes on a culture that is becoming increasingly autonomous.

Up until the mid-twentieth century, the idea that the dominant culture was a form of secularized Christianity was taken for granted. As we shall see, radical French secularists espoused the same anthropological view of the family as the one propounded by the Church. Assuredly, the nineteenth century is one of conflict between the Catholic Church and manifestations of 'modernism', but the moral doctrine of traditional French secularists, starting with Jules Ferry,[20] did not differ substantially from the moral doctrine defended by the Church. The conflict between the two was to do with power and the source of values; in other words, it was about truth. Everything changed in the 1960s, springing from two simultaneous movements: the *aggiornamento* (updating),

Catholicism's reconciliation with modernism brought about by Vatican II, and the revolution in morality that took place in that decade. This is what truly initiated dechristianization, which is not so much a decline in religious practice as a reference to a new anthropology centred on human freedom. But before arriving at that discussion, let us return to the conflict between Christianity and secularism in the nineteenth century.

3

Another Source of Morality?
The Church Versus Modernism (1864-1964)

It took the Catholic Church a century (from 1864, when the *Syllabus Errorum* was issued, to 1965, the end of Vatican II) to complete its *aggiornamento* and abandon its objective to impose its version of truth. This was a century of tension, even conflict, but also one of misunderstanding between the Church and European states. The quarrels affected all of Europe, and they all resulted in disqualifying religion as the source of shared values, although in different ways. Ultimately, in the 1960s, they produced another divorce between Catholicism and secularism, which this time pertained not to the source of values but to the very definition of what is good. Prior to the 1960s, the Church was at odds with the secular powers over the questions 'Who is the source of the truth?' and 'What is the pillar and foundation of truth?' After the 1960s, the nature of the conflict changed, and the question became 'What is "good"?'

The Philosophy of the Enlightenment and the Secularization of Moral Doctrine

After the Enlightenment, moral values were no longer derived from divine authority. Without necessarily denying the existence of God, the movement's thinkers sought to deduce morality from reason. Descartes posited the fundamental autonomy of the subject (*cogito*), an essential philosophical act of the Enlightenment. Kant defined a rigorous and rational morality without ever bringing in God as a hypothesis. The existence of God became a postulate of practical reason; it 'completed' morality but was not its foundation. When secular rationalism entered politics with the French Revolution, French secularists claimed to be just as moral as believers, even arguing that their convictions were all the more solid as they were not motivated by the fear of God. For them, there were not two versions of morality, but a single one. The Church is in agreement on this point (natural morality is merely the reflection of Christian morality). What was debated was not moral values themselves, but rather their foundation. As Marcel Gauchet and Rémi Brague have both noted, modern society believes that it has founded itself.[1]

The introduction of non-denominational schools, for instance, implied that 'ethics' be taught without reference to God. Most European countries thus underwent de facto secularization; even if there was no separation from the church, teaching everywhere came under the control of an education ministry, and, for this ministry, religious teaching became a subject area among others. In short, the independence of morality from religion is not only a consequence of a new philosophy, it is also the result of the autonomy of the secular state, which had to define and teach civic ethics with no point of reference that superseded the state. The question of morals naturally becomes crucial when the state takes over public education.

In France, secularization of the education system took place in a context of conflict,[2] with the Jules Ferry Laws of 1882 mandating compulsory and secular education, rounded off with the Law on the Separation of Church and State in 1905. But all over Europe, whatever the relation between church and state, secularization became inevitable as soon as the state took over responsibility for civil society instead of delegating it to churches.

To fully grasp the issue, it is worth rereading Jules Ferry's 'Letter to Schoolteachers', written by the minister of public instruction just after the law creating mandatory secular education was enacted. Jules Ferry assigned teachers the mission of giving pupils 'moral and civic instruction' and imparting to the children 'those simple rules of moral conduct which are not less universally accepted than the rules of language or of arithmetic'. He prescribed the 'secular teaching of morality' and not the 'teaching of secular morality', and so did not contrast 'secular morality' with 'religious morality', clearly considering morality to be

45

universal. This has not been understood by those today who advocate teaching a 'secular morality' in school. Ferry wrote:

Properly speaking, you have nothing new to teach, nothing which is not familiar to you as well as to all honest men. Thus when people speak of your mission and your apostolate, do not misunderstand: You are in no way sent forth with a new Gospel; our legislators did not wish to make of you either a philosopher or an improvised theologian. […] Speak, therefore, to [the] child as you would like [a teacher] to talk to your own [children], with force and authority, whenever it concerns a question of undisputed truth or a precept of common morality; with the greatest reserve, as soon as you risk touching upon a religious sentiment of which you are not the judge.

And he suggested a practical guideline:

Ask yourself if a father, nay, if even one single father, present in your classroom and listening to you, could in good faith disapprove of what he heard. If so, refrain from saying it. If not, speak fearlessly, for what you are going to impart to the child is not your own wisdom; it is the wisdom of the human race; it is one of those universally accepted ideas that centuries of civilization have added to the heritage of humanity.

In a word, no religious parent could be shocked by what the secular schoolteacher would say, because, according to Ferry, both shared the same value system. There was in fact nothing revolutionary about Jules Ferry's morality: to justify his system, he mentioned 'the good sense of the father and the heart of the mother', drawing on the religious notion of the complementarity of the sexes. For him, secular morality embodied the same standards and values as Christian morality; the only difference was that it had now been rationalized and stripped of superstition and fear.

For nearly a century, up until the 1960s, Europe's republicans would champion the same conservative values as the Catholic Church, at least with regard to matters of the family, women's status, abortion, and homosexuality. This morality was 'secularized' in civil and penal codes under different names: 'offence against morality', 'public order', 'breach of decency', or the famous injunction in French law to act 'as a good father' ('*en bon père de famille*'), the analogue of the 'reasonable person' in English law. In the civil marriage service, spouses pledged to be faithful to one another and the wife owed obedience to her husband; the man was consistently defined as the 'head of household', and children born outside of marriage did not have the same status as legitimate ones (even if this had more to do with property transmission than with Christian morality). Rare tensions emerged over divorce, which was not truly legalized in Catholic countries until the 1960s, but even elsewhere civil divorce was based on the concept of 'fault', including adultery, which is a secularization of sin. And although the communist left were strong advocates of a freer lifestyle, they did not call the family into question and were wary of excessive sexual freedom. They believed the bourgeoisie had loose morals, whereas the working class was 'healthy', as illustrated in Bernardo Bertolucci's film *1900*, produced in 1976, and by the stance taken by Jeannette Vermeersch, activist and wife of the French Communist Party secretary-general, against birth control, which in 1956 she described as 'a weapon in the hands of the bourgeoisie against social legislation'.

The Catholic Church's Reaction Against Modernism

The tougher line taken by the Catholic Church in the mid-nineteenth century therefore did not arise from a conflict over values. Thomism, instituted as the official doctrine of the Church by Leo XIII's encyclical *Æterni Patris*, issued in 1879, granted the idea of a natural law and morality shared by both believers and non-believers, and accepted that there was no contradiction between faith and reason. In the eyes of the Church, the rejection of 'modernism' pertained to two essential points: its role in society (and hence the question of its relationship to the state) and its authority in matters of values.

The first conflict was political. It pitted the Church not only against secular and anticlerical forces but also against conservative states that professed to be Christian. Let us mention the most significant ones: Spain, with the forced sale of the Church's mortmain properties in the first half of the nineteenth century; Switzerland, with the Sonderbund

War in 1847, in which a confederacy of Catholic and conservative cantons was defeated by the federal state, the consequence being the expulsion of the Jesuits and, later, strict limitations on the opening of episcopal sees (this was perhaps the last war of religion in Europe, although it claimed few victims); Italy, the unification of which brought an end to the Papal States and their army with the capture of Rome in 1870; Germany, with Bismarck's measures against the Catholic Church between 1871 and 1878 (an episode known by the premonitory name of *Kulturkampf*, 'culture struggle'); France, where republican anticlericalism, which held sway especially from 1881 to 1914, peaked with the Law on the Separation of Church and State in 1905, which was rejected by Pope Pius X; the United Kingdom, where the Catholic Church refused to compromise with the Anglican Church, the state church. Another example is Pope Benedict XIII's condemnation in 1899 of the 'Americanist' current of the Catholic Church in the United States, which attempted to reconcile Catholicism and the liberal values of American society.[3]

Politically, the Church initially condemned the separation of church and state. It actively protested after the capture of Rome in 1870; the *Non expedit* decree issued in 1868 forbade Catholics from participating in the Italian elections, and was not lifted until 1919. In France, the Church rejected the Law of 1905, whereas the majority of French bishops were in favour of a compromise.[4] The

Church wholly identified with General Franco's Spanish nationalists, giving its blessing to the bloody repression of the republicans. Thus, at first, it refused to stop being an institution that intervened directly in society and political life. Gradually, and reluctantly, the Church would finally learn its lesson from the failure of its hard-line stance. It agreed to delegate intervention in the political sphere to Catholic laity, via the Catholic Centre Party in Germany, founded in 1870, and later the Italian People's Party, established in 1919.[5] Finally, after considerable reticence toward Christian democracy (whose greatest faults were its independence from the Catholic hierarchy and its secularism, even though its members were believers), the Church ended up viewing this trend as an instrument of political influence, to the point of openly forming an alliance with the Christian Democracy party in Italy from 1946 to the party's collapse in 1994.[6]

Up until the First World War, the Church had two enemies: political liberalism (democracy) and theological relativism (tolerance). With regard to the latter, the Church was really defending its monopoly on truth, not only in religion but also as pertained to anything that had to do with morality and values. The various encyclicals are clear on this point: the Church was not willing to allow its magisterium to be questioned.

In the examples mentioned above of conflicts between church and state, the issue is not so much one of values as one of authority, or about their foundation and what justifies them. When, as with the *Kulturkampf*, church and state were at odds over civil marriage, it was not the definition of the family that was at stake but control over civil society. In places where the Church was powerful divorce was not legal. However, it is worth noting that the ban on abortion at the time was backed by nationalists and not the Church—in France, it was the National Bloc that in 1920 strengthened laws against contraception and abortion, which the Napoleonic Code had already criminalized in 1810, and for the same reasons: to encourage a rise in the birth rate so as to produce more soldiers. More generally speaking, when feminists in the suffragette movement began protesting for the right to vote, it was not the Church that opposed them, but indeed virtually the whole spectrum of political forces. As for homosexuality, it was criminalized just about everywhere in Europe. This was even more the case in Protestant countries than in Catholic countries, due to the fact that in the former, the secular state took responsibility for values—in Germany, the United Kingdom, the Netherlands, Denmark, Norway and Finland homosexuality was still illegal after 1945, whereas in France and Italy it was generally dealt with under 'offence against morality'.

Despite this de facto convergence of values and the Church's acceptance of the idea of universal natural law, for nearly a century the Catholic Church was adamantly opposed to the secularization of morality, which by definition implied that its magisterium was no longer required to define good and evil. Doubtless there was a kind of natural law, but it could only be fully realized by recognizing the truth, otherwise society would descend into moral relativism. The Catholic Church's offensive was about what constituted the foundation of values, in both political and moral terms—a foundation that it held could not depend on human freedom. Popes rejected the very idea of moral progress and freedom of thought, not to mention religious relativism. Pius IX (1846–78) and Pius X (1903–14) wrote several encyclicals and apostolic letters explicitly denouncing liberalism and modernism. The Church claimed not only that there could be no secular morality but also that there was only one religious truth: its own. In other words, there can be no equivalence among religions (including Protestantism and Orthodoxy, cf. the encyclical *Pascendi* of 1907). The Church upheld the doctrine of Biblical inerrancy—that the Bible cannot err in matters of faith— though it did not reject historical or philological exegesis.

Of the major texts in this struggle, which would lead to the 'modernism' crisis at the turn of the twentieth century, Gregory XVI's (1831–46) encyclical *Mirari Vos* (1832) came first. It condemned all democratic freedoms and all new rights, which would eventually become known as 'human rights'. Severed from the authority of the Church, it claimed, freedoms (referred to as 'license') would undermine the whole social order, and everything would collapse into anarchy, violence, and revolution—in short, the apocalypse. Next came Pius IX's encyclical *Quanta cura* (1864), which stated that 'where religion has been removed from civil society […], the very notion of justice and human rights is darkened and lost.' Annexed to this was the *Syllabus Errorum*, a list of things considered anathema by the pope; among these was the need to separate church and state. Then, in 1870, the First Vatican Council proclaimed papal infallibility in matters of doctrine. Leo XIII (1878–1903), regarded as more open, asserted Biblical inerrancy (even if he encouraged exegesis) in *Providentissimus Deus*, issued in 1893. Pius X's apostolic constitution *Lamentabili sane exitu* (1907) condemned sixty-five modernist propositions attributed to French priest Alfred Loisy, who would be excommunicated in 1908.

From 1910, all clergy were required to take the Antimodernist Oath, which was not abolished until 1967.[7] At the same time, the encyclical letter *Vehementer nos* vigorously condemned the French Law of Separation of 1905; in particular, it criticized the fact that religious organizations established by the law were not subject to the hierarchical structure of the Catholic Church, and thus escaped the authority of bishops and the pope. The law was amended in 1923 to recognize bishops' supervision of priests.

Once again, the content of values was not in question. All that mattered to the Church was that its authority not be disputed. Protestant churches would not have this problem, since for them the only issue is the convergence of two types of morality: religious and secular. By definition, Protestants reject the magisterium of a church that claims to have a monopoly on truth. Opposition to secular states, a rather rare phenomenon among Protestants, occurred either in the name of God's absolute transcendence (in the tradition of Karl Barth)—which is beyond 'morality'—or, paradoxically, in the name of a 'theology of the secular world', such as put forward by Dietrich Bonhoeffer (1906–45), who was executed by the Nazis. But in both cases, Protestant churches did not enter into competition with the state, whose prerogatives are recognized. The Catholic Church therefore remains the focus of our analysis of the tensions around secularization.

The blend of conflict and complicity was illustrated by Giovannino Guareschi in the *Mondo Piccolo* stories, which formed the basis for the famous series of *Don Camillo* films in the 1950s and 1960s (with Fernandel as the Catholic priest Don Camillo). In western France, as in northern Italy, two societies coexisted: the parish with its youth groups, and the Protestant church with its youth fellowships. Each had its own social institutions: football clubs, annual dances (people had to reproduce!), cinema clubs, summer camps, and conferences. 'Mixed' marriages were rare. The issue, as Gramsci determined, was indeed one of cultural hegemony. But while the two camps were political opposites, they concurred in their opposition to the secular ideologies of Fascism and Nazism (the Catholic conservative right, which was allied with Italian Fascism, paid for this upon Liberation in 1945).

Vatican II seemed to have resolved the conflict. Not only did it endorse secularization, but it practically made of it a new opportunity for the Church. However, there would soon be a new and deeper rift, as believers and secularists ceased to share the same values. In the late 1960s, the Catholic conservative right made its comeback.

4

The Self-Secularization of Religion

The Church Enters the Modern Era

The Church's transition to modernity did not initially occur by way of theological reform. It came about through pastoral and missionary praxis as well as the rise in power of lay Christian actors: between two popes known for their intransigence (Pius IX, who decreed papal infallibility, and Pius X, who condemned 'modernism'), Pope Leo XIII, without compromising on any religious dogma, opened the way for the Church to engage with secular politics. In 1890, by inviting French Cardinal Lavigerie to raise a toast to the Republic before a gathering of naval officers (who were French, but hardly republican—it is not by chance that the French navy is dubbed 'La Royale'), Leo XIII tacitly recognized the Republic, and thereby the autonomy of the political sphere. This was also done explicitly in the encyclical written in French *Au milieu des sollicitudes* (*Inter sollicitudines*) on 16 February 1892. Similarly, Leo XIII took into account the 'social question', acknowledging that people were no longer living in a traditional society. If the Church did not want to lose its pastoral and universal vocation, it would be important to address the emergence of a working class developing outside of the parish framework and increasingly subject to the appeal of 'socialism'. The Church's social doctrine, set forth in the encyclical *Rerum novarum* (the very title of which acknowledges that the Church was faced with something new: modernity was a fact, even if its negative effects were lamented), defined the basic principles of what would become the Catholic Action movement.

The issue was no longer to bring the faithful back to church. The Church now had to reach out to secular society, which meant organizing open, socially oriented pastoral work (Catholic Action) and using secular political instruments, in other words what was to become Christian democracy, which no longer required religious observance but simple adherence to secularized Christian values. The Church delegated political action to a 'secular arm', so to speak. This encouragement to engage in social action fostered the emergence of what would be called 'progressive Christians': it began with the worker-priest movement[1] after the Second World War and peaked in the 1960s, when left-leaning Christians took part in the sweeping movement to emancipate minds and peoples, hand in hand with other progressive activists. In Vatican II these Christians would find a Council that revamped theology and especially the liturgy. They advocated action over theology, even if some offered theological justifications for progressivism, such as Father Cardonnel in France, Father Gustavo Gutiérrez in Latin America, who promoted liberation theology in the late 1960s, and Dom Hélder Câmara, bishop of Recife, Brazil, champion not only of the poor but also of the liberation theologians condemned by John Paul II and Cardinal Ratzinger in Rome in the 1980s.

The Church's new approach to politics had its ups and downs, from the condemnation of Action Française in 1927 to the banning of worker-priests in 1954, but it went on for nearly a century. It was matched by a segment of the missionary movement that engaged in a new approach to indigenous cultures, as mentioned previously: inculturation. Pius XII also encouraged the development of an indigenous clergy, trained according to the same curriculum as European priests but careful not to appear as a conveyance channel of the colonial authorities: this 'indigenization' would contribute to shifting the centre of Christianity away from Europe.

It hardly needs to be said that there were rising tensions, between a more open praxis—favourable to welcoming a sort of secularity that there was no longer any use in denying—and a theology that remained focused on ritual, the seven sacraments, worship and prayer. This tension eventually resulted in Vatican II, which adapted theology and especially religious rites to the modern world, acknowledged by the Church at long last.

The Protestant World

Aside from the Catholics, other denominations would also become involved in the social and political sphere. In Protestant countries, believers became actively involved in trade unions and left-wing parties, such as the Labour Party in the UK. But the relationship to secularism was and remains, as we have seen, very different among Protestants.

Protestant Europe did not experience a *Kulturkampf* as the vast majority of Protestant churches had 'self-secularized' by the nineteenth century. Under the influence of, among others, the German theologian Friedrich Schleiermacher (1768–1834), they abandoned all pretence of contesting the established political authority, barring a few episodes (like Dietrich Bonhoeffer's confessing Lutheran Church, a small minority church that opposed Nazism). The Protestants found themselves siding with the Swiss federal state against the Sonderbund; with Bismarck during the *Kulturkampf* (even if many encouraged reconciliation); with the secularists in France, before and after the Law of 1905; and finally with Italian independence.

This fusion into a liberalism that was often more ethical than religious was contested by various 'awakening' movements, and prompted the emergence of small dissident churches that broke away from the dominant churches (particularly in the Netherlands and Norway, where they revived an old English tradition of dissenting churches). But in Europe, fundamentalist Protestant sects remained on the sidelines of politics, while revivalist movements often injected an extra measure of soul into what would become trade unionism and social democracy in Protestant countries.

Starting in the 1960s, there was a fundamentalist and charismatic revival in European Protestantism. It initially arrived as an American import, even if it has undeniably taken root today. The first community to be affected were the 'Travellers' in the 1950s, with the Gypsy Evangelical Mission (Mission Évangélique des Tziganes de France), founded in 1952 by Pastor Le Cossec, a Breton Catholic who had converted to Pentecostalism, immediately placing him on the fringe of the Protestant establishment. In the meantime, this late-twentieth-century revivalism was sweeping the Third World, particularly Africa. The African, Chinese and Tamil immigrant diasporas in Europe were strongly influenced by evangelical 'missionaries' who now came from the Global South. These Protestant fundamentalists did not involve themselves in politics, which is largely explained by the fact that, unlike the evangelicals in the Americas, they often recruited among immigrant populations, who did not identify with Christian Europe. Their depoliticization did not, however, prevent them from condemning abortion and same-sex marriage, but they did so without taking part in street demonstrations organized principally by Catholic movements. These Protestants are fairly indifferent to the theme of Europe's Christian identity, because for them it is neither a matter of identity, nor a question of Europe; it is instead an issue of faith, and of the entire world.

Thus, while Protestants in the United States (in particular the Southern Baptists) were the vanguard of the 'culture war' (which, despite its name, was concerned with values and not culture), in which they were only joined by conservative Catholics later, in Europe it was the Catholic Church that was against the transformation of values in European society from the time of the protests of 1968 onwards, without ever being joined by a significant number of Protestants.[2]

The dominant trend in European Protestantism is the self-secularization of the religious sphere, both in terms of morals—the best of Christianity resides in ethics, which are universal—and in terms of theology—God reveals himself in the profane. After Schleiermacher and the nineteenth-century liberal theologians (such as Adolf von Harnack), Dietrich Bonhoeffer, in his rather allusive letters from prison, would evoke a 'non-religious Christianity', in which faith is radically stripped of the trappings (and crutches) of 'religion'. If God was real, then he was among the non-believers, too. Religion was its own separate space, but God could not be apart. Bonhoeffer rejected the 'two kingdoms' doctrine that Lutheranism had advanced to sanctify obedience to temporal powers—this theory, or political theology, was used to justify a passive attitude to Nazism. Bonhoeffer viewed political involvement as a religious duty, not for the sake of any particular church and its norms, but in the name of shared values.[3] For Harvey Cox (b. 1929), whose influential book *The Secular City: Secularization and Urbanization in Theological Perspective* was published in 1965, it was important to follow the 'ethos of the modern world': secularization was an opportunity for humankind to finally achieve maturity and not believe out of fear or compulsion. For Cox, God is at work even in secularization; He is the Lord of History before being Lord of the Church, and secularization is part of his plan. The Church should therefore take the lead at the head of the secular movement.

Cox's view is thus completely at odds with the notion of a faith community besieged by secularism. Like Bonhoeffer, he holds that believing in God is about 'caring for others'. Ethics take primacy over theology, and even over faith. The 'theology of encounter' prevails over the theology of truth. The consequences of this view are clear: European Protestants had little trouble accepting, or at least tolerating, the right to abortion and same-sex marriage.

The Theological Reform of Vatican II

For global Catholicism, the Second Vatican Council (1962–65) hailed the adaptation of theology and ritual to modernism, ending a decades-long fight. Some have described it as a Protestant approach, or a Catholic version of the self-secularization of religion.

Ever since, God has spoken in 'secular' vernacular languages. Priests dress like everyone else, while many push for an end to clerical celibacy; churches no longer have steeples and blend into the modern urban landscape. The switch to vernacular languages tamed the dogmatic vigour of Latin.[4] Hell was emptied of inhabitants, at least in the hereafter; here on Earth it became 'other people', according to Jean-Paul Sartre. There was much more than *aggiornamento* at stake. While fundamental theology has remained the same (the *Credo*; the dual nature of Christ, human and divine; faith in the resurrection of the dead; Christ's presence in the Eucharist, etc.), the sacraments have been reinterpreted in a more 'contractual' and participative spirit, and the ritual takes place according to a watered-down liturgy that is more reassuring, one in which love prevails over fear. This has happened alongside desacralization, which is much more far-reaching than the mere switch away from Latin. In other words, this switch introduced a theological shift, and a new form of religiosity, but without the solemnity of an explicit declaration.

The conversion from Latin to vernacular languages goes beyond the matter of translation: in French, it entailed a theological re-evaluation or reorientation. In sermons, for instance, the devil steps back, even disappears. The sacrament of penance becomes that of 'reconciliation'.[5] 'Extreme unction' becomes the 'anointing of the sick', and instead of preparing the soul for passing, the hope of an earthly cure or improvement is expressed. In any case, it is life here on Earth that matters. In the sacrament of marriage, the passage from the Epistle to the Ephesians demanding the wife's submission to her husband is hardly ever read anymore. As a logical consequence of the Church's new theological approach to Judaism highlighted by Vatican II, certain prayers have disappeared from the new liturgy, such as the Good Friday prayer for the conversion of the Jews (*Oremus et pro perfidis Judaeis*).[6] The liturgical reform has implicitly diminished the role of the clergy in favour of the role of the layman: in performing rites, rather than looking east toward the 'Light of Christ' with his back to the worshippers, the priest now faces the congregation, which participates. Traditionalists criticize the active participation of the faithful, as well as the desacralization inherent in the act of receiving communion while standing, rather than on one's knees. Even more lambasted are those priests who take the liberty of freely altering the official translation of certain prayers and invocations, as if the literal translations fall short of the mark.

At the same time, the proximity between priest and congregation reduces the specific importance of the separated clergy as spokesmen for the Church in favour of the participating community of the faithful. One might also ask why the priest should remain celibate (separate) at all if he must immerse himself in the world to propagate the values of faith. Clerical celibacy has in fact become a recurrent question and is discussed within the Church, even if John Paul II refused to open up debate on the topic. Since

Vatican II, many priests have indeed married and 'left the ministry', to use the Church's expression.

Moreover, the famous Pastoral Constitution issued at the end of the Council, *Gaudium et Spes*, mentions 'the rightful autonomy of the creature'.[7] The creature is respectable and should be respected, even if autonomy does not mean detachment from the Creator of all things. Promotion of the secular—of earthly affairs—also naturally leads to a certain desacralization. The very idea of an absolute truth that dominates everything on Earth is set aside. What religion contributes to social anthropology in terms of sexuality, for instance, is a measure of sensitivity (for it does not question the family structure described by social anthropology), the idea that sex is not only a matter of reproduction but that it is the act of love. Millenarianism descends to Earth: social justice is possible, and for the most radical, liberation theology makes it possible to theorize the revolution and collective salvation together.

Is this the sanctification of the secular or the secularization of religion? It is the triumph of secularism, through what Jürgen Habermas calls a 'translation' process. Since secularists no longer understand anything about the sacred and find the faithful to be strange at best, fanatical at worst, if the religious hope to live with their convictions peacefully within a secularized society, they must translate them into the secularist's language. Bishops and theologians must therefore be bilingual: to be able to speak in 'lay' terms in public and reserve the 'religious' talk for an often empty church.

The effect on society has been predictable: the anticlericalism inherent in Westphalian republicanism is gradually fading. 'Secularists' are no longer violently anticlerical. The object of their ire is now the fundamentalists, such as French Catholic archbishop Marcel Lefebvre, who set up a schismatic organization, the Society of Saint Pius X, in 1970. They like 'good popes', such as John XXIII and Francis, and decry reactionary popes who might forget Vatican II, like John Paul II and Benedict XVI. In addition to criticism, they now heap opprobrium on John Paul II for turning a blind eye to the widespread and rampant paedophilia among the clergy. Pope John XXIII was without a doubt the first pope to be immensely popular among non-believers (he was equally so among the believers, but it is relatively common for a pastor to be loved by his flock). Secular Europe applauded the Council and was delighted by the great reconciliation between Christianity and Europe's cherished modernity. Modernity had been acknowledged by Protestantism and Judaism, and now came the turn of the Catholic Church.

Of course, there remain a few curmudgeons, the fundamentalists who reject the theological ratification of liberal modernity, such as the Society of Saint Pius X founded by Archbishop Lefebvre, to which also belong the occupants of Saint-Nicolas-du-Chardonnet Church in Paris, openly affiliated with the far right. But at a time when Islam was beginning to make its appearance on the European stage, Vatican II offered a means to counter all sorts of fundamentalism (which would soon bring about the Iranian revolution of 1979) with a Christianity of openness, tolerance and love. Christian identity and the values of modernity were no longer in contradiction. Leftist Catholics could finally feel they were in step with history.

This evolution was in general widely appreciated by the public, who chose 'openness' and were happy when a 'good pope' imposed courageous reforms of the reactionary curia. This public were ready to fight for the right for divorced and remarried people to receive the Eucharist, or for priests to marry.[8] They hand out points to Francis when he welcomes immigrants, inveigh against him when he reiterates that abortion is not permitted, and scratch their heads when he says he believes that Satan exists.

By invoking its *aggiornamento* during the Second Vatican Council, the Church wondered how it could develop a ministry of welcome in a society that had become religiously illiterate. The authors of the French Law on the Separation of Church and State were perfectly familiar with the Church: some of them, such as Émile Combes, were former seminarians. If these laymen who made the Law of 1905 had been asked to define transubstantiation, communion, or the Trinity, most of them would have answered without hesitation. But the last of the religiously literate French presidents was François Mitterrand (there is uncertainty about Emmanuel Macron). Today's society is characterized by widespread religious illiteracy. If a person in the street is asked who the three persons of the Trinity are, it is highly possible that he or she might answer 'Mary, Jesus and God'. It would be a wasted effort to ask the meaning of the Eucharist, as well as many other terms familiar in Catholic culture prior to Vatican II.

Yet, the Church's *aggiornamento*, which aroused both considerable admiration in public opinion and a state of tension in traditionalist circles, did not produce the anticipated religious reawakening or revival in terms of practice. It was soon followed by another crisis in relations between secularized society and the Church. This is because right when the Church decided to adapt to the modern world, the modern world was experiencing considerable upheaval, as a new value system emerged out of what has been called 'the spirit of the 1960s'.

The paradox is thus that just when the Church had accepted a secular civil society, the common values of society drifted away from those of the Church.

5

The Turning Point of the 1960s

The 1960s were a key period, comparable to the years following the publication of Luther's *95 Theses* in 1517. After Vatican II and the triumph of religion's self-secularization came the encyclical *Humanæ vitæ* in 1968, advocating a maximalist position forbidding any sexual activity not intended for procreation (except 'the rhythm method'). Catholics did not understand this position that had seemingly come out of the blue. Secularists were outraged at the reactionary pope. Why, when the Church Council had elaborated a theology of modernity, would Pope Paul VI reaffirm traditional norms?

He did so because he realized there had been a radical change in shared values, meaning that 'natural' law and morality were no longer in accordance. Society's values were no longer secularized Christian values; new values had been founded on individualism, freedom and the valorization of desire. Personal freedom prevails over all transcendent standards. There is no longer a natural morality common to all. Thus, Christian values made their comeback in the form of explicit moral norms precisely because they were no longer understood and shared by all. Yet, as we will see, culture itself is today being reformulated as a system of explicit moral norms.

The Crisis of 1968 and the Anthropological Turning Point: A New European Culture

At a time when the Church and secular society seemed to have reconciled over the defence of common values, as Jules Ferry suggested, both in a secularized form and in the form of religious norms (dignity, solidarity, love, abnegation, the gift of self, etc.), the 1960s witnessed the affirmation of a new anthropological paradigm that shattered this common base.

A wave of youth revolts swept through the world during the ten years between 1963 and 1973: the Chinese Cultural Revolution; the JVP insurrection of youth in Sri Lanka; the protest and massacre of students in Mexico City; and similar phenomena in Kabul, and in Japan (the Zengakuren movements).[1] Even if these movements usually professed solidarity with the working class, they were autonomous, generational and aroused considerable distrust within traditional Marxist parties, which held that generation could in no way be a substitute for class. I will not go into the political dimension of these movements here.

The strictly political aspect of events in May 1968 in France soon evaporated—even if it lent fluidity to the left–

right dichotomy—facilitating the transition to libertarian neoliberalism. The revolution was dead, but radical political protest was not, even if it would bizarrely become territorialized and confined to specific urban centres, from Madrid to Paris, and rural areas (from the farmers' Fight for the Larzac to anti-airport protests at Notre-Dame-des-Landes; from the Italian NO TAV movements against the Lyon–Turin high-speed railway line to the protests against the renovation of Stuttgart train station). The consequence is that the far left is failing to oppose globalization, offering no new universalist perspective and leaving national politics to right-wing populism.

What is interesting here is that in Western Europe and the United States these youth movements brought about a radical change in the system of dominant values (at least with regard to sexuality and the family), which gradually became enshrined in law everywhere over the fifty years that followed 1968. The fact that the law, in the form of legislation or court decisions, ended up giving legal existence to the new values shows that they are now dominant in European culture. In this regard, there was not a 'conservative reaction' to May 1968 in terms of values. The populism that mounted in the late 1970s was not really a counterrevolution, because the object of its hatred (elites, immigration, the European Union) is not the new value system. Populism is just as individualistic, hedonistic and anti-elite as young people were in 1968; the only difference is that populists seek their pleasure solely among themselves.

Any succinct overview of 'the Sixties model' would have to begin, of course, with its valorization of individual freedom, a legacy of the Enlightenment. This was extended to the realm of desire, which became a standard in itself and was no longer subject to any constraint other than the desire of others. The problem, which would take longer to resolve, is the harmony of desires. For the philosophy of the Sixties and the movements inspired by it, this harmony is taken for granted: children, for instance, were at that time also presumed to feel desire. Sixties culture was fundamentally libertarian in this sense. In more recent times, however, the popular spread of the #MeToo movement and outrage over paedophilia in the Church do not represent reversions to puritanism as much as they are attempts to prevent desire from being used to justify power relations or predatory relationships. This explains why conservative Catholic circles have resisted joining these two movements aimed at placing limits on sexual desire, even though they might have been expected to jump at the chance of settling their accounts with the legacy of the Sixties.

Another new aspect of Sixties culture is the valorization of nature in all respects—one's own body, instinct and the environment—as opposed to the tradition of the free exploitation of nature, attributed to the capitalist system. Environmentalism, vegetarianism, organic food and alternative medicine all fit in with this logic. But the paradox is that renouncing the Promethean myth of man's dominion over nature stops at the human body. On the contrary, the body is the very object of individual freedom: my body is my business. There is a continuity between the demand for birth control, assisted reproductive technology, transgenderism, and the contemporary fascination with neuroscience. Sixties culture introduced a new relationship with nature, which is seen as intrinsically good without recourse to any norm (there is no 'morality of nature'), and which is therefore malleable and can shift according to human will.

The increasing prominence of gender fluidity is another noteworthy development. The appearance of the term 'gender' is itself a sign; there is a growing movement against assigning a gender (that is, the categories of 'man' and 'woman') according to sexual or social characteristics, as gender is no longer defined as natural but is seen as cultural, and implies a predefined social role. Of course, all cultures delineate sexual categories and assign to them more or less fixed social roles. Now, however, the very notion of gender allocation, whether biological or cultural, is being contested. The individual's choice takes precedence, and the very notion of category, and hence of culture, disappears.

In fact, the revolution that began in 1968 was not about asking for women's equality, which feminists have demanded for centuries, from the French Revolution to Simone de

Beauvoir, but instead was about rejecting the very fact of gender assignment. Here, the biological is denied, but it is not replaced by culture, because culture itself is accused of perpetuating gender inequality. Gender fluidity and the destruction of a gender binary are seen as the way forward to rule out the domination of men over women.

The Institutionalization of Sixties 'Values'

It is important to realize that the change in the system of norms and values did not just impact society and behaviour, it also entered law—a process that took place over fifty years and, once again, at different paces in different countries. These developments were not necessarily associated with left-wing majority governments, even if the right is assumed to be more conservative. In France, under the presidency of centrist Valéry Giscard d'Estaing (1974–81), abortion was legalized and family law was also modified, introducing divorce by mutual consent (removing the need for 'fault'); equal rights for children born out of wedlock; and spousal equality in the choice of place of residence and right to a working life. The trend continued with simple statutory declaration of divorce in 2018. In Italy, divorce, which was only allowed for the first time in 1970, was made simpler by laws in 2014 and 2015, though it nevertheless remains subject to a fairly lengthy process. Ireland went from constitutional criminalization of abortion in 1983 to legalization in 2018, with a nearly identical margin in both referendums. Everywhere there have been changes in marital laws in the direction of equality between husbands and wives in terms of residence, adultery, 'obedience' and, more recently, parental leave. It is worth remembering that in Ireland in the 1960s, a female civil servant who married would lose her job, as only 'heads of household' worked. Meanwhile in France, a husband would only be committing adultery if he brought his lover into the marital home.

In 2001, the Netherlands became the first country in the world to legalize same-sex marriage, followed by Belgium in 2003 and Spain in 2005. Once again, the distinction between Catholic Europe and Protestant Europe no longer has any meaning. Moreover, in Europe, while gay marriage has usually been legalized by left-wing parliaments, the right does not attempt to overturn these laws when it takes power, meaning that a consensus generally ends up taking hold. Little by little, the very definitions of sexual difference, family, reproduction and parenthood have been redrawn, but not as part of the agenda of any specific political party. Though governments might show some reluctance at first, in general they accept and enshrine the population's evolving mores. Opinion polls play an important role here, making governments aware of tipping points in public opinion.

Reproduction has also been redefined. The old Roman legal maxim '*Pater est quem nuptiæ demonstrant*' ('He is the father whom marriage indicates to be so') has been replaced by two different and contradictory elements. First is an obsession with biological origin, made possible since the discovery of DNA; in Danish law, for instance, finding the biological father is obligatory for registering a birth.[2] Everywhere, secrets of this nature are spilling out of family closets—in the liberal press, from *The Guardian* to *L'Obs*, a new journalistic genre has even developed: 'How I discovered my true family ancestry'; 'My father wasn't my father'; 'I found out my sister was actually my mother', etc. At the same time, there are demands to legalize assisted reproduction methods that totally disregard biological parenthood and obliterate the status of donors and surrogate mothers, only recognizing parts of their bodies: sperm, eggs and wombs.

In short, there is a tension between a totally biological perspective on parenthood on one hand, which would lead to the disappearance of anonymous birth registration and call into question full adoption, which does away with biological kinship, and on the other hand the total individualization of procreation, in which parenthood becomes merely contractual. The new 'family' thus functions according to two different paradigms: nature on one hand, with genetics (and its corollary, evolution) at the centre, and demiurgy on the other hand (I create what I want to). The first paradigm is profoundly deterministic, the second fundamentally libertarian. Without getting into value judgments about artificial procreation, the system is unstable in terms of a 'source of values'.

In any case, the 1960s must not be remembered as a mere hedonistic craze during which society was briefly consumed by the pleasure principle. The revolts of 1968 marked a complete anthropological revolution, whose values are today enshrined in law and deployed in rigorous codes of human relations. This is not to say that the period produced a new form of puritanism. The Sixties revolution brought about new moral norms precisely because it broke with the previously dominant culture, and hence the rules of society needed to be clarified. Changes had to be made to the limits of freedom. The most exemplary case is that of paedophilia: while for a time it was almost seen as acceptable,[3] after a period of turbulence and hesitation it has come to represent absolute horror. One of the greatest errors of the Catholic Church, which is far from the sole institution to be implicated, is in its failure to understand that in the space of two decades a 'venial' sin had turned into a 'mortal' or capital sin.

This shift in relation to paedophilia does not mean that there has been a backlash or a counter-revolution against the Sixties, or a return to the moral status quo ante. Those who are the most critical of the #MeToo movement and its demand for limits on male desire are the same former puritans who were against same-sex marriage. In opposition to #BalanceTonPorc (the French version of #MeToo), Christine Boutin, the only MP representing a Christian party, spoke out in favour of rehabilitating 'French cheekiness',[4] in other words, a game between norms and transgression, grounded in cultural convention.

To return to the theme of Christian Europe, the biggest paradox remains that, at the very moment the Church had adapted its theology to the modern world, it went to war against modernity's new values. This was not, however, with the aim of setting back the clock and returning to 'the good old days'. For the Church is not concerned with culture, but only with moral norms in the absolute, according to what it holds to be the truth.

6

The Religious Secession
The Encyclical *Humanæ vitæ* (July 1968)

A Turning Point for Sexual Norms

In July 1968 the encyclical *Humanæ vitæ* was issued, imposing on Catholics a stringent code of sexual morality in line with Pius XI's 1930 encyclical *Casti connubii*, or 'chastity in marriage'. In particular, *Humanæ vitæ* rejected all forms of artificial contraception.

Where did this bombshell come from? Many Christians were expecting the Church to adapt to the tide of sexual liberation, but instead, just when birth control pills appeared on the European market, hence proposing an alternative to abortion, the pope issued an encyclical taking a stance against the changing mores. Sexual morality came to be the newest battlefront between religion and Europe's dominant culture, and became central to the way of life promoted by the Church.

The encyclical was important for two reasons. First, it proclaimed the Church's rejection of the values of freedom

81

and hedonism favoured by the 1960s youth movement, thus marking the end of what the public at large and many Christians perceived as an attempt to adapt to secularization and new values, as the Second Vatican Council had done. Second, it ushered in a new era in which the Church would counter secular society with a system of norms revolving around sex, and therefore the family and procreation, and implicitly the status and place of women in the Church and in society. Notably, this system was reformulated in terms that were also acceptable to non-Catholic conservatives, such as being 'pro-life' and believing in 'true love'.

In an address to the European Parliament in 2006, Pope Benedict XVI listed the 'non-negotiable moral issues' in the eyes of the Catholic Church (contraception was not among them, as it does not come under state control):

> Protection of life in all its stages, from the first moment of conception until natural death; recognition and promotion of the natural structure of the family as a union between a man and a woman based on marriage; … the protection of the right of parents to educate their children.

He continued:

> These principles are not truths of faith, even though they receive further light and confirmation from faith; they are inscribed in human nature itself and therefore they are common to all humanity. The Church's action in promoting them is therefore not confessional in character, but is

addressed to all people, prescinding from any religious affiliation they may have. On the contrary, such action is all the more necessary the more these principles are denied or misunderstood, because this constitutes an offence against the truth of the human person, a grave wound inflicted onto justice itself.[1]

This position has become the Church's leitmotiv since the 1980s, and has not been challenged by Benedict XVI's successor, Francis. Each time they meet with politicians, European bishops repeat the same thing over again, even when the circumstances are inappropriate.[2] This is not out of simple puritanism or moralism: this normativity is rooted in a system of natural law, which the Church claims to defend against the new dominant culture in European civil society. Time and again, it pits 'truth' against relativism. For the Church, European society is no longer merely profane; it has become pagan, even 'Christianophobic'.[3] By turning its back on what the Church calls the 'culture of life', in other words the prohibition of abortion and the centrality of reproduction in the natural framework of the family, society had become immersed in a 'culture of death'.[4] For the pope, European civilization had become nihilistic out of hedonism and, after the pleasure-seeking phase of the 1960s, it had inevitably developed a sort of death cult, evidenced by a morbid fascination for Satanism, a rise in suicide rates and youth violence. The rift between Catholicism and dominant European culture no longer had to do with power. It also went well beyond a disagreement over morality. It had become an anthropological question: what was society in general, and European society in particular, founded on?

In the fifty years that would follow, despite Pope Francis' vague gestures of openness, like the Synod on the Family in 2015–16 (which, nonetheless, ultimately rejected communion for remarried divorcees to all intents and purposes, and hardly addressed the issue of homosexuality), the Catholic Church in Europe as well as evangelical Protestants in the United States would make sexual norms, from abortion to the definition of family, the backbone of their relationship with the state and civil society. Other subjects, such as defining what is 'good' in politics, social issues, the economy, solidarity, immigration, or even pastoral ministry, seemed secondary.[5]

What once bridged the gap between believers and non-believers, namely a shared base of secularized Christian values, had faded or disappeared. The consequences of this ran deep, and ushered in a new world in which faith communities are—and definitely believe themselves to be—beleaguered minorities, even if a segment of the conservative Catholic right still dreams of reconquest by riding the populist wave. But this raises more serious questions. If the Church no longer recognizes the dominant culture in Europe today as Christian, who would take the liberty of claiming that Europe's identity is Christian? And how could this Christian identity be reclaimed without a battle for

Europe's morals, which would be directed less against Islam (which often shares the same family values promoted by the Church) than against European society itself?

Not only does this change the position of the Catholic Church but it also alters the very meaning of what it is to be a believer in Europe.[6] Religion has not made a 'comeback'; as we have seen, all measures confirm the decline in religious practice. However, in many ways religion has become more visible precisely because it is no longer part of everyday life. Its 'soft' forms (occasional church attendance, or superficial conformity to religious norms) have vanished due to secularization and self-secularization, in particular among traditional Protestants (Lutherans, Anglicans and French and Swiss Protestants). The 'new priests' don the cassock, but, unlike Abbé Pierre or countryside priests before the Second World War, they wear it as a token and not as a marker of their occupation. One displays one's Christianity. The campaign by French secularists to eliminate from the public sphere religious symbols that were accepted fifty years ago is not only because Islam has arrived on the scene. It is also because the meaning of these Christian symbols has changed. They have become signs of activism, a way of bearing witness, rather than cultural or professional symbols. This is why the imposition of public displays of the crucifix in countries that don't share France's *laïcité* (for example, Italy and Germany) is controversial. Instead of being the expression of a traditional culture deeply infused with Christianity, these symbols today seem to indicate a desire for reconquest, or to display identity markers in the face of Islam, especially when they are promoted by secular authorities, a prime example being the case of the Bavarian government in 2018.[7]

Once again, if I seem to grant the Catholic Church a virtual monopoly on Christian expression, it is because the major Protestant churches in Europe have been self-secularized, as we have seen, and have attempted to integrate new paradigms into their theology, such as the ordination of gay ministers or religious services for gay marriages, which dilute them even more in secularized society. Religions that refuse to self-secularize, on the other hand, redefine themselves as communities of faith in which 'real' believers gather, whether born again or converts. These believers build their lives around religion and perceive themselves as a minority within a secularized Europe—a minority that is besieged, both by Muslims and secular culture, but that also wants to proselytize and convert Europe back to Christianity.

Catholic Revivalism

However, far from all being fundamentalists,[8] Christian revivalists comprise a fairly large spectrum of positions and forms of spirituality. The most 'traditionalist' are characterized by their desire to revert to Latin mass and the wearing of the cassock. In politics, they might be close to the far right. But their focus is usually on strict observance of the rites of mass, perhaps in a 'retraditionalized' form, with a portion in Latin; on the role of the priest as intercessor between the believer and God;[9] and on the return to ways of worship somewhat neglected after Vatican II.[10] It is also worth mentioning the charismatic practices borrowed from American Protestant revivalism, which involve expressive movement of the human body, or which are more oriented toward spirituality, placing an emphasis on the meeting of an individual and Christ, lived faith, feelings, emotions, renewing baptism vows, and the importance of community practice outside of mass, such as in prayer groups and through meditation, in which the clergy plays a more minor role. These approaches are not mutually exclusive, which is why the portmanteau 'tradismatic' has been coined to describe the entire trend.[11] It should be viewed as a broad spectrum, ranging from a more traditionalist pole to one that is fully charismatic.

The most traditional communities (such as the Community of Saint-Martin) are clearly clergy-centred: they reassert the central role of priests in the Church and emphasize their training and a return to more traditional forms of mass. The most charismatic communities, meanwhile, offer the laity the opportunity to live 'as a community' in which the priest is not at the centre of their practice (such as the Focolare Movement or Communion and Liberation in Italy, or the Emmanuel and Chemin Neuf communities in France).[12] Most tradismatic communities are not oriented toward the outside world and devote themselves instead to spiritual rebirth within the Church, without, however, neglecting charity and social work. The only charismatic movement that defines its mission as 'serving others'—and also the only one that is left of the political centre—is the Community of Sant'Egidio.[13]

These communities all have something in common: they are deterritorialized. They have taken advantage of the status of 'institutions of pontifical right', which depend exclusively on the Vatican, do not come under the authority of the bishop where they are established, and are often supranational.[14] In this type of religious community, one is either in or out; often one must take vows, sign a contract, and truly commit oneself. But while the commitment is restrictive, the degree and form of membership are variable. These communities include priests and laity, and among the latter, men and women, married couples and single people, who, as families or as individuals, choose communitarian or ordinary lifestyles, punctuated by rallies and meetings. Some, like the Emmanuel Community, may be led by laypersons for a set period. All, however, perceive the secular world as pagan, rather than merely 'profane'.

Above all, their deterritorialization accentuates the split between these faith communities and the rest of society, because they no longer share the same space. Two parallel worlds have formed that no longer have common values. For believers only faith matters, whereas people in the secular world have lost all basic knowledge of religion and thus find the faithful to be a bit weird at best, fanatics at worst.

The grey areas described by sociologists of religion (regular practice, irregular, occasional, and so on) no longer exist. Believers do not identify with the values that have become dominant in society and have a tendency to insist on what distinguishes them. Meanwhile, those who do not practise, despite still identifying as 'Christians', no longer have a religious culture: they know neither the dogma, the rites, nor the technical vocabulary of religion—from 'altar' to 'concupiscence' to 'tabernacle', and of course other less common words—which they often find abstruse. Traditional forms of organized religion, which are usually territorial and therefore local, such as the parish organized around a priest who lives there, are in crisis, not only due to a lack of priests but also because the very concept of 'nominal Christian' is disappearing. Baptism in a parish once automatically entitled a person to the benefits of the Church, as it was customary to marry in the church where one was born. But as of the 1980s, young priests have arrived on the scene who have taken to asking engaged couples if they indeed belong to the 'community' at all, since they have never been seen at Sunday mass or anywhere else.

The Reconfiguration of European Catholicism

Christianity, whether Catholic of Protestant, has been restructured by these charismatic tendencies. Rather than culture or identity, personal faith has become the core of faith communities, which are no longer necessarily territorially based. Individuals attend the church where their sympathies lie. Religious affiliation is no longer just one aspect of social life but is at the centre of the believer's life. Members of these faith communities are not on a cultural quest. They are not interested in culture or institutionalized religion. Theirs is an individual, in some cases individualist, quest, alongside peers travelling the same spiritual road. Without quite reaching the level of anti-intellectualism dominant among evangelical Protestants, the new Catholic faithful have also distanced themselves from culture—a result of their quest for a direct relationship with God and of the valorization of emotion to the detriment of knowledge.[15]

Moreover, one might wonder if ritual for Catholics does not fulfil the same role as emotion for Pentecostalists. In any case, prayer groups such as the Catholic Mothers Prayers, by making a priest's presence superfluous, bring the two confessions closer together.[16] The return to tradition among European Catholics, which should have placed the priest back at the centre of praxis, has paradoxically been accompanied by a rise in the laity. The importance of deacons[17] has widely grown. Movements such as Focolari, Sant'Egidio, and Alpha course groups are led by laypersons, even if priests are members, while Christian philosophers, such as Rémi Brague, in some instances play a more important role than theologians. And yet this sociological shift toward the laity has not been ratified by a reform of their status in the Church.

John Paul II and Benedict XVI were very much in favour of the establishment of these new institutions of pontifical right, while many bishops who came out of Vatican II were more hesitant, as the communities largely escaped their control. But little by little, bishops emerged from the ranks of these communities, such as Dominique Rey and Marc Aillet in France and Cardinal Angelo Scola, patriarch of Venice and then archbishop of Milan. Consequently, the influence of these tradismatic movements in the Church today is out of proportion with their actual membership; not only are they among the most committed, and thus most visible, groups in the Church, but they also play a considerable role in the recruitment and training of priests and the lay Catholic elite. Their diversity and the variety of religious sensibilities they represent offer a far broader range of choice than what is generally labelled 'fundamentalist'. For example, while the Community of Saint Martin remains closed to other cultures and religions, Cardinal Scola, a member of Communion and Liberation, is very involved in discussions with Islam through the Oasis International Foundation, which he founded.

It is important to note that the influence of these communities also comes from a lack of dynamism from other parts of the Catholic Church. The Catholic left has virtually disappeared, or has been reduced to a few small groups that can barely make themselves heard.[18] Among the long list of reasons for their demise are the crisis of the left in general; the disappearance of their sociological base; Catholic Action's gradual swing toward more charismatic forms; the crisis in the humanist culture shared by believers and non-believers alike; and especially what I have called the self-secularization of religion, that is, the translation of the message of the Gospel into secular terms (ethics, liberation, solidarity), which resulted in the loss of a truly spiritual collective. In short, one might say that leftist Christians now feel out of place in secular society and in the Church—in society because they are left-leaning, and in the Church because they are not interested in outward displays of piety, and especially because, ever since John Paul II, the Church has been unwilling to give the laity, and especially the female laity, the place they demand.

The status of ordinary parishes is more complex. Believers who go to mass nearly every Sunday not only define themselves as practising Catholics but they are also not necessarily tempted by tradismatic tendencies. It is true that the number of practising parishioners has plunged all over Europe over the past fifty years and that the group is aging, but they are still there. They are characterized by a strong territorial attachment to the parish where they attend church, and do not like to have their habits shaken up. But there is no longer a priest for every parish. Only two pools exist, therefore, that might renew this framework: African priests and tradismatic clerics (the two categories, of course, may coincide). The arrival of an African priest in a rural parish where the populist or extreme right vote is on the rise may well provoke some teeth-gritting, but everything really depends on the personal chemistry between the cleric (who might also be European—Polish, for example) and his worshippers. The arrival of priests who belong to tradismatic communities (like the Community of Saint Martin, in the case of France) is much more of a game-changer.

There are a few case studies available. The example of the Basque Country is particularly interesting for two reasons: the shift towards a more conservative and charismatic form of religiosity, and the relationship to a deeply grounded local Basque culture.[19] Marc Aillet, a priest of the Community of Saint Martin and the bishop of Bayonne since 2008, no longer seeks to appoint Basque-speaking priests on the pretext that all Basques understand French. This is a superb example of deculturation and the view that language is a mere tool for communication, not a vehicle of cultural identity. Bishop Aillet has sidelined traditional Basque church choirs because their repertoire is too profane, but he does not hesitate to invite Brazilian evangelical choirs who sing the love of Jesus Christ. The cultural (and I would add, aesthetic) loss is obvious.

Today, priests and diocese officials are recruited on the basis of their religious leanings and sensibilities. Relations outside the Church, with town halls, other confessions, artistic and folkloric circles, and secular intellectuals, are increasingly distant, or even more fraught. Outward displays of faith abound—church processions have returned and there is overt participation in political debate to defend Benedict XVI's 'non-negotiable moral issues'. More than ever, the Church refers to an anthropology inspired by Thomas Aquinas which supposes that natural law is the expression of divine law, hence it bans same-sex marriage; this theology is explicitly espoused by the Community of Saint Martin. The Church openly criticizes society's dominant culture, and in particular all that pertains to LGBT rights and visibility.

These new trends emerged among Christians back in the 1960s, and not always in reaction to Vatican II. At the time, believers were influenced by American charismatic evangelicalism; the search for Christian communities (in parallel with post-1968 communes); the role of charismatic personalities (such as Chiara Lubich for the Focolari); the end of the illusion that 'everything is political' (to which part of Catholic Action had succumbed); and so on. From the moment he became head of the Church in 1978, Pope John Paul II used the various charismatic networks of the time as the main instrument in his transformation of the Church. What was at first only a sensibility thus gradually became official Vatican policy, which Benedict XVI went on to pursue. The aim was to break not only with progressivism but also with everything that involved compromising with secular society on the Church's essential values. The Church no longer needed the Christian democrat laity as intermediaries in order to converse with the outside world. It assumed the roles of preacher and rebuker itself.

At the same time, the Church did not call into question the separation of church and state, which it had previously endorsed.[20] Still, it fought against worldwide secularization in its discourse by appealing directly to the lifeblood of society: young people. World Youth Days are the most publicized and well-known manifestation of the new, young face of the Church. They function on charisma in both senses of the word: John Paul II's personal charisma and young people's direct spiritual experiences. Behind all the pomp there has also been a renewal of the clergy worldwide, as the upper age limit for bishops was enforced to appoint a raft of new cardinals (usually without fanfare). John Paul II drew from a new generation of priests, such as André Vingt-Trois to replace Cardinal Lustiger in Paris; Amédée Grab to replace Archbishop Haas in the diocese of Chur, Switzerland; José Cardoso Sobrinho to succeed Dom Hélder Câmara in Recife, Brazil; and two bishops from Opus Dei as successors to Archbishop Rivera y Damas and Archbishop Óscar A. Romero in San Salvador. In fact, all over Latin America 'reactionary' bishops were appointed as the generation of conciliar bishops disappeared—in Chile, Argentina, Peru, Colombia (with Lopez Trujillo) and Brazil. It should be noted that the appointment of several of these bishops created highly conflictual situations between the priests and the laity in their dioceses, in particular the case of Wolfgang Haas in Chur.

Even though Pope John Paul II was a European, as was his successor Benedict XVI, his policies would paradoxically marginalize Europe by pushing universalism and the deterritorialization of the Church. Under his papacy, institutions of pontifical right—both faith communities and clerical institutes—were encouraged and proliferated, sometimes against all reason, such as the Legion of Christ in Mexico, whose founder Marcial Maciel Degollado was the subject of countless notorious scandals, including numerous cases of sexual abuse, but remained close to the pope until the end.[21] During his papacy, John Paul II made forty-eight trips outside of Europe, out of just over a hundred trips abroad altogether. On all his trips he addressed the people directly and spoke to heads of state as an equal. The Vatican set about minimizing the role of the laity as an intermediary in its interactions with states and societies, precisely because the very concept of 'intermediary' diminished the impact of the message of faith. The Church wanted to speak in its own name, while claiming a monopoly on Christian representation in Europe. Its entire relationship to politics had been altered, as we shall see below.

The End of Christian Democracy

The Church's repositioning in favour of a militant, uncompromising religiosity had an immediate impact on the political sphere. Admittedly, it did not revert to the anti-modernist intransigence of the nineteenth century, but it began to directly admonish states, politicians and institutions in order to defend Benedict XVI's 'non-negotiable moral issues', all of which revolve around upholding an anthropological model founded on natural law.

Christian democracy, which the Church had previously instrumentalized in order to have a hand in politics, had therefore become useless for three reasons. First, the Church no longer claims to have a say in the full range of human activity, such as the economy and political institutions, but only in its core norms and values. Second, the Church has reaffirmed its clericalism (a layperson cannot stand in for a priest) and therefore cannot delegate politics to an autonomous secular body, even one under its influence. Third, Christian democracy was once by definition a locus of compromise where the boundary between believers and non-believers dissolves, as it does not request a baptism certificate of its voters or even of its leaders.

Christian democracy grew out of the realization that it would not be politically expedient to create a 'Catholic party', and that it was important to recognize the separation of church and state and bring people together regardless of their religious affiliation. It defended a form of secularized

Christianity that professed to subscribe to the Church's social doctrine, that is, the rejection of communism and unbridled economic liberalism in the name of justice, personal dignity, solidarity and subsidiarity. It was thus just as Catholic as Protestant and was open to electoral alliances. It shared an important feature with social democracy: the defence of the welfare state (to which could be added the promotion of popular culture and involvement in the social and trade union arenas). The development of Christian democracy from 1945 to the 1970s is evidence that the Church's first adaptations to the modern world, and particularly its political participation, were in motion well before the theological modernizations of Vatican II.[22]

The demise of Christian democracy was the result of the erosion in the 1960s of secularized Christian morals in European culture. Christian democracy would survive a few more years before finally foundering. In Italy it sank into corruption, perhaps due to the disappearance of everything that justified its existence and formed its ideals. In some countries, such as Germany, it self-secularized; in others, it has been replaced by parties on the conservative right that can no longer claim to be Christian, like Forza Italia in Italy and Partido Popular in Spain. In something of a paradox, Catholic figures who were formerly Christian democrats have shifted to the centre left: in Italy Matteo Renzi's government was comprised of more practising Catholics than the previous right-wing administration under

Berlusconi and the following populist government of Salvini and Di Maio. When Angela Merkel, leader of the German Christian Democratic Union, attempted to appeal to the Christian values of tolerance and welcoming strangers during the refugee crisis in 2016, her words went down badly even within her own party.

The Church and the Dilemma of the Political Link

Under John Paul II and Benedict XVI, the Church embarked upon a new mode of political intervention, focusing on the non-negotiable moral issues (against abortion, euthanasia, same-sex marriage, artificial procreation) without proposing a comprehensive view of society. By stepping up its lobbying efforts directed at political elites[23] and mobilizing an activist base, it attempts to exert pressure on leaders regarding these specific issues. It no longer holds back from allowing Christians to mobilize on the street; Cardinal Barbarin, among others, encouraged people to join the Manif Pour Tous demonstrations against gay marriage in France. It is noteworthy that the secular state of France is bearing the most visible witness to the political radicalization of conservative Catholics, with La Manif Pour Tous; Les Veilleurs (The Watchmen), who hold high-visibility prayer sessions outside government buildings; and the bishop of Fréjus' discreet backing of Marion Maréchal, Marine Le Pen's niece, who has distanced herself from her aunt's secularism in an attempt to develop a Christian populism.

The problem is that by deciding to focus only on sexual morality and family, a small segment of the Christian way of life, the Church—at least until Pope Francis—has lost sight of other Christian values. This narrow focus also results in short-term political choices that tend to lend support for populist movements. These movements do have a comprehensive vision for society, but it is one that is very different from the view of the Church.

However, while rightly noting that Europe is no longer Christian, Popes John Paul II and Benedict XVI nonetheless remained extremely attached to the idea of Christian Europe, and hence to its reconquest. For them, if Europe is no longer Christian, it is not because secularism has rejected faith but because it has turned its back on natural law. Moreover, whereas the charismatic movements evince complete indifference to culture,[24] Popes John Paul II and Benedict XVI were very attuned to Christianity's hold on the culture of a nation or a people. Yet their policies essentially amounted to institutionalizing the rift between the Church and the dominant culture they deplored. Here we enter into one of the deep contradictions of the new ministry, for the universalism that characterizes the charismatic movement in fact perfectly suits a church that has lost its sway over actual societies and that finds in a globalized world the ideal space to regain its autonomy (as it did in the sixteenth century with colonization, and in the nineteenth with the abolition of the Church's concordat with various states). But how can this universalism be reconciled with the desire for rootedness and inculturation, which alone are able to re-establish the link between the Church and a society that has lost faith? How can faith and identity be reconciled?

The question therefore arises of whether a Christian Europe is conceivable outside the clerical institution. Moreover, the Church must ask whether it can ally itself with populists whose relationship to Christianity is purely identity-based, even if their values conflict, particularly when their attachment to Benedict XVI's 'non-negotiable moral issues' is highly doubtful.

7

Identity and Values
Europe and the Other

Culture Wars: The Case of the United States

In Europe, 'values' have probably never before been mentioned so frequently in discourse and political debates as they have since the 2000s. As mentioned in chapter 4, this trend actually dates to the American 'culture wars', which have been going on since the 1970s. The term, popularized by James D. Hunter's book,[1] does not refer to Samuel Huntington's 'clash of civilizations',[2] which appeared in print a few years later. The expression 'culture wars' denotes the war on values within American society, a war pitting liberal culture, which stands against discrimination and in favour of abortion rights, gun control and some form of social security, against a 'Christian right' led by evangelical Protestants in the southern United States, whose core political issues are the fight against abortion and same-sex marriage, and who oppose gun control, universal health care, immigration and affirmative action. The conservative wing of the Catholic

Church in the US, strengthened by the new bishops appointed by John Paul II, quickly joined this coalition, but it has confined itself primarily to the issues of abortion and same-sex marriage, while keeping quiet on immigration (which brings Catholics into the country), gun control and social security.[3] Of course, there are also many practising Christians in the ranks of the liberal or progressive movement, but they have not managed to come together to form an independent Christian social or political coalition.

Every US election since Ronald Reagan came into office in 1980 has revolved around this values war, pitting two increasingly divided Americas against each other. Huntington's clash of civilizations thesis shifted the fault lines in 1996 by situating the battle outside the framework of American culture and reframing it as a clash between Western culture and the other (Latino immigrants, Muslims, etc). The election of Donald Trump in 2016 highlighted the close connection between anti-immigration (and anti-Islam) factions and the Christian right, which have long been linked, especially as there are no atheistic or even secular populist movements in the US, apart from a few marginal neo-Nazi groups. These voters want to both stop immigration and ban abortion. Rejection of Islam has played a major role, uniting evangelicals, including a strand of 'Christian Zionists' that does not exist in Europe,[4] with anti-immigrant groups, despite the fact that immigration from Muslim countries is very low in the US and that

Huntington himself viewed not Muslims but Mexicans (despite their being Christian) as America's main cultural threat. To put it simply, in the war of values there are only two camps, as is clear in each election: the 'liberals' (including many Christians) and evangelical Christian populists. The internal front over values and the external front over immigration and Islam dovetail.

Europe's Culture Wars

Things are more complex in Europe because the two fronts do not coincide. In the debate on values, the internal front pits Christian conservatives against secularists of all persuasions, liberals and populists alike; the main issues revolve around abortion and same-sex marriage. The external front, on the other hand, puts the idea of 'Europe' in opposition to Islam: the issue is concerned with the cultural antagonism between Muslim immigrants and Europeans and with European societies' fear of becoming 'Islamized'. The two fronts do not map onto each other. Although the base of practising Catholics has often slid toward anti-immigrant populism, the Church is careful not to endorse this shift, even if it is highly equivocal about the matter of Europe's Christian identity. In effect, a rift has opened between those who advocate welcoming migrants, and those who reject what they see as Islam's entrenchment in Europe. The Church is fighting over values but does not, at least in principle, reject immigration; on the contrary, we know how much Pope Francis insists on welcoming immigrants—although this elicits protestations, or worse, from some conservative Catholics. Conversely, many secularists who support the right to abortion and same-sex marriage are opposed to Islam for the same reasons they are opposed to the Catholic Church and religion in general (the *Charlie Hebdo* line). Lastly, populists see immigration as their priority, but remain discreet about the question of values due to the fact that they are divided between liberals, who espouse the values of the 1960s (like Geert Wilders in the Netherlands), and conservative, homophobic anti-feminists (such as Matteo Salvini in Italy).

European populism took off by criticizing immigration and putting the spotlight on Huntington's clash of cultures, not by addressing the issue of values specific to European society. The first slogan touted by the Front National in France, a forerunner in this regard in 1978, went as follows: 'One million unemployed is one million immigrants too many'.[5] Far-right parties that grew out of pre-war fascism—in France, Italy (with Fratelli d'Italia), Austria, Sweden and Germany—thus gradually put their historic influences to one side and 'modernized' by seizing on the issue of migration and making it the centrepiece of their propaganda, thereby finding a means to cover up their own history (not to mention their anti-Semitism). But, starting in the late 1990s, a reaction to the relationship between immigration and Islam in Europe started to grow (unlike in the US, where, as discussed, immigration is mainly Latin American). Populist parties emerged *sui generis*, without fascist roots and built solely on the basis of opposition to immigration and Islam. This is the case in the Netherlands, Denmark, Norway, Switzerland, Germany (with Pegida), the United Kingdom and Italy (with the Lega Nord). These parties are not only purely secular—like the former fascists in fact, who are often fascinated by neo-pagan theories— but they have also usually embraced the new liberal culture in terms of mores and have incorporated much of the social-democratic programme, particularly regarding the welfare state.[6]

There is another obvious difference with the US, namely that in Europe, the Catholic Church, and not the Protestants, is at the vanguard of the battle for values. Europe's main Protestant churches have largely adopted new values—most Lutheran churches perform homosexual marriages and do not condemn abortion. Meanwhile, Protestant evangelicals, recently imported to Europe, have for the time being remained discreet in the public and especially the political arena; given that they position themselves as a global movement and that a large majority of their adherents come from immigrant backgrounds, the question of Europe's identity is irrelevant to them. However, unlike southern US evangelicals, the Catholic Church in Europe has always kept its distance from populist movements and the far right, and this is for several reasons. First of all, it views the values of charity and populist egoism as opposites, and fears that if populism extols Christian identity, it will be to the detriment of the religious message. Second, it considers itself universal, not linked to a specific ethnic or national group. Last, it is distrustful of the more or less rampant paganism in a segment of the identitarian far right.[7] This wariness has nothing to do with an alignment with 'progressives'. In France, the bishop who has taken the strongest stand against the Front National is Cardinal Barbarin, a leading figure in the fight against same-sex marriage.[8]

The hierarchical structure of Catholicism long enabled the Church to keep its 'centre-right' flock in all countries where it had an influence on their vote: France, Italy, Germany, Portugal, Spain and, to a lesser extent, Austria. But in Belgium, ever since the linguistic crises of the 1960s, in which the Church was unable to rise above the fray (the Catholic University of Leuven was partitioned into two universities in 1970, one French and one Flemish), its ability to wield authority over the Catholics was already being beaten back. Polls show that in 2015, the taboo around the far right was lifting almost everywhere across the practising Catholic electorate, not least because the demise of Christian democracy left no natural option for a Catholic vote. The collapse of the taboo has not only been due to the Church's loss of influence but also because of constantly mounting internal tensions, which are no longer related to the conservative vs progressive division that was born of Vatican

II. Lastly, while the Church as a whole (no matter what one might say about Pope Francis' supposed liberalism) is holding firm to its positions in the war of values, the inroads Islam has made in Europe have brought about a re-examination of the question of identity, which features at the heart of the populists' political programme.

The Debate over Christian Identity

When a constitution for Europe was being drafted in 2004, an important question was raised: should the treaty enshrine the principle of Europe's Christian identity by making reference to the continent's 'Christian roots'? The request came from Christian MEPs who wanted to rectify what they saw as an omission on the part of the European Union's founding fathers. But while the suggestion was ultimately rejected (not least because of France's refusal to endorse it, in the name of *laïcité*), the debate went on, and gained momentum. Three currents are in conflict:

- The Church, for which a reference to Christian roots would primarily have been a way of entrenching its values in Europe's very definition. The Church is concerned with both Christian identity and Christian values, and as well as pushing for constitutional recognition of the continent's Christian roots, it actively lobbies Brussels to defend the 'non-negotiable moral issues'.

- Populist parties and movements, for whom the main issue is to resist Islam. They defend Christian identity for identity's sake, without emphasizing values, but speak about national or regional identity rather than Europe itself.

- The 'secularists' (the '*laïques*' in France) who, while sometimes acknowledging Europe's Christian heritage, emphasize the Enlightenment, human rights and the achievements of the 1960s: sexual liberation, contraception, abortion, gender equality, feminism, and LGBT rights. These are the people who talk about 'European values' (or 'republican values' for the French) as opposed to religious norms in general, which are deemed backward or contrary to human rights. They perceive Islam as an intensified contemporary form of the religious absolutism that Europe fought against and vanquished in the past.

The boundaries between these three groups often blur because the 'populist' category is extremely heterogeneous. Populists are united only by their obsession with Islam, criticism of elites, and defence of a unified 'people' with a common—anti-European—identity. Populism has a Christian pole, like the Polish PiS, and Marine Le Pen's niece Marion Maréchal,[9] and a secularist pole, encompassing most of the populists in Northern Europe. Among the latter group is the Netherlands' Geert Wilders, who represents the most liberal wing of populism in terms of social mores, and the most repressive toward Islam, which he wants to outlaw outright. There has also been a noticeable shift toward populism among left-leaning and politically liberal intellectuals, who are motivated by national sovereignty and an obsessive fixation on Islam.

The Church Between Identity and Values

As we have seen, John Paul II and Benedict XVI were strongly attached to the concept of a Christian Europe. Both wanted to reconcile faith and identity, but using the former as a starting point. For them, there was no inherent opposition between identity and values; even though identity is a matter of fact, whereas values concern intention, the 'fact' of identity cannot hold without faith. The two popes saw values, since they are confirmed by natural law, as the bridge between faith and identity, but also as something spiritual that can only be offered by faith, and not by identity. Identity—or nature or natural law—is too weak and too unstable a notion from which to derive 'true' values. This is why these popes did not believe secular intermediaries, such as Christian democrat parties, could be relied upon to ensure the perpetuation of essential values.

For Benedict XVI, as for his predecessor, recalling Europe's 'Christian roots' was a way of inciting Europeans to return to Christian values, and if not a return to religious practice, then at least greater respect for religion and the message it stands for. For the Church, this does not mean encouraging nostalgia but undertaking the spiritual reconquest of Europe. We will later examine the Church's reaction to populists' demands to display cultural signs of Christianity in order to counter what they call the Islamization of the public sphere. For the Catholic Church, not only is it futile to conceive of a Christian Europe outside of the institution of the clergy, but siding with populists is problematic to say the least, especially when their relationship to Christianity is solely based on identity and often conflicts with the Church's values, from Benedict XVI's 'non-negotiable moral issues', to the sensitive issue of the reception of refugees.[10]

The Church's Attitude Toward Islam

Meanwhile, Islam's arrival in Europe has placed it in a somewhat ambiguous position for the Church. Islam embodies religious dynamism and has reintroduced religion into the public space. Many of its believers outwardly practise their religion and challenge the authorities to take their faith into account. At the same time, Islam's presence in Europe calls into question the continent's Christian identity, and more importantly poses as a serious competitor for its spiritual reconquest. If the Church maintains an interfaith dialogue, it is obviously not in order to reach some sort of minimal theological compromise, grounded, for instance, on the notion of 'Abrahamic religion'. It is rather to ease tensions, and sometimes to set up an ad hoc 'common interfaith front' to combat measures deemed unacceptable; such was the case with the joint Catholic, Protestant, Jewish and Muslim declaration against same-sex marriage in Lyon in 2007.[11] However, the Church is doing little to normalize this kind of coalition. Interfaith marriages, for instance, are not encouraged, even between Christians.

In other words, the Church does not mind giving Muslims a folding chair in European society, but certainly not a real seat. After all, there is only one *Sancta Sedes*, or Holy See. The Church's ambition is not to eradicate Islam but to assert its own rank, which has been jeopardized by secularization and the series of scandals among the clergy in the past twenty years. This is nothing new. The same policy was directed at the Jews, Protestants and the Orthodox, and then, too, had more to do with tolerance than a concern for equal rights.

This is evident in the Church's position on building mosques, which it does not oppose per se. Until the 1980s, it even lent or donated church buildings to Muslims. But in general, the Church opposes grand mosques—such as the grand mosque planned in Florence (which does have a grand synagogue)—while backing neighbourhood mosques. Military chaplaincies are another example of tolerance and not equality; in every country they are held by the dominant religious group. Even in France, where one might think secularism would impose equality of religion, the Catholic

Church has an army bishop, whereas the three minority religions have to make do with a 'head chaplain' (no army rabbi or military imam). In private, Catholic officials readily criticize the lack of theological sophistication of their Muslims counterparts, a shortcoming ascribed sometimes to their mediocre intellectual training, sometimes to Islam itself. In short, for the Church, while it is important to defend Muslims' right to practice their faith, it cannot accept the equality of religions in Europe. Here, like everywhere else, the Church rejects religious relativism.

The Church and the Secular Offensive

The problem for the Church and Christians in general is less Islam than the rise of two other forces: populism and secularism. These developments have caused a de facto shrinking of the religious space. Populism has essentially reduced religion to folklore, whereas the secular offensive continues to expel religion from the public space. By focusing on defending a normative anthropological model that opposes Sixties values—by fighting, for example, against abortion and same-sex marriage—the Church has been prompted to take a fragmentary approach (opting for strict adherence to the norm combined with a dose of charity) and to make reactive choices without having a vision for the long term. It has provided no spiritual response to the broader trends of populism and secularization. Furthermore, the Church has developed a siege mentality, especially since it is dogged by paedophilia scandals. For years it perceived these accusations as a vicious smear campaign, until summer 2018, when a barrage of new revelations of sexual abuse emerged in the US, Australia, Chile, and across the globe, forcing the Catholic Church to face the facts.

The Church's ambitions to convert Europeans en masse back to Christianity now seem like a pipe dream, since secularism has carried the day. Even if mass reconversion is attainable, it certainly will not be brought about by the Church's current policy on the normative fronts, which acts more as a hindrance. Since the Catholic Church rejects the self-secularization practised by Protestantism, it is thus left with three other possible routes.

First, there is the option of political combat to enshrine Benedict XVI's non-negotiable moral issues in law as much as possible. If the Church is unable to make a convincing case for its moral norms, it must impose them by law, and therefore have as much legislation passed as possible to limit abortion, same-sex marriage and new forms of artificial procreation and assisted death. In doing so, while it might like to see itself as the world's conscience, the Church actually acts like its policeman.[12]

The example of Ireland indicates the limits of this option, and time will tell its success in Poland in years to come. While for the Church this strategy derives from belief in divine values, civil society, which refers to other values, secular and hedonistic, views it simply as the imposition of an authoritarian moral code, one that seems increasingly hypocritical as the extent of sex and financial scandals within the Catholic Church continues to be revealed. In such conditions, the Church will find populists to be even less amenable as political allies than Christian democrats, since even the conservative wing of populism does not reject the new values fought by the Church. The gap is therefore widening between a combative Church and the public, which, especially in the wake of the paedophilia scandal and the Church's doublespeak, could revert—and is already reverting—to the good old anticlericalism of the nineteenth century.

The second route for the Church is 'the Benedict option', to quote the title of a popular book among conservative Catholics in the US.[13] The book's subtitle—'A Strategy for Christians in a Post-Christian Nation'—makes the issue even clearer. According to the author, Christians are a minority in a pagan, even barbarian world, just as they were in the sixteenth century when Saint Benedict established the first monasteries for community life (as opposed to the solitary life of hermits and anchorites). The book argues that Christians today should live among themselves in modern monasteries, where they would follow their own rules while waiting for divine Providence to restore belief on earth. If one bears in mind that Benedictine monasteries came into being as the Roman

Empire fell at the hands of the Barbarians, the underlying comparison is easy to see: secularism and Islam are two facets of a new barbarian state.

The final option for the Church is spiritual reconquest. This stems from the same observation—that we have returned to the time of paganism and the Barbarians—but instead of closing in on themselves, Christians should embark on converting the pagan world through preaching. Everywhere is mission territory, and proselytes should address not only 'former Christians' but also Muslims. In an interview with *Le Monde* newspaper the new bishop of Paris, Michel Aupetit, made a statement in this regard, which, oddly, did not attract attention:

> The question of Islam frightens people because of the terrorist attacks and discourses maintaining that France will become a land of Islam—we are back to the issue of cultural insecurity. But we have experienced other cultural insecurities in the past. Geneviève, patron saint of Paris, lived at the time of Attila the Hun and Childeric, king of the Franks. The Germans and the Franks who arrived were not at all part of the Gallo-Roman culture or the Christian culture. It was a colossal transition. At the time, the Church prioritized an evangelical culture, even if that meant sacrificing its Roman culture. That period, far worse than our current era, also made us what we are.

The message is very clear: identity has no place. The barbarian should be converted to Christianity, even at the price of our own deculturation. Religion has to rebuild itself, without paying heed to culture.[14]

At a time when many conservatives are preoccupied with the comparison between the Fall of the Roman Empire and the supposed decadence of the modern West, Aupetit's statement[15] rejects what serves as the very foundation of populism: nostalgic identity. His message is a feature of the conservative or neoconservative charismatic movement.

Christian Secular Identity and Populism

Europe's Christian identity is a recurrent theme among populists. It is insisted upon in Catholic areas in particular, but is also a cause among many secularists and some Protestants too. But, when they speak of Christian identity, are populists really talking about the Christianity of the Church? Populists could in fact make this remark of Montaigne's their motto: 'We are Christians as we are Perigordians or Germans.'[16] Christianity then is no longer a religion, but an identity.

For the populist right currently riding high in the polls in Europe, the fight against abortion is not an electoral priority. This segment of the right now views sexual freedom—and in northern Europe, even feminism and same-sex marriage—as an aspect of European identity that separates Europeans from Muslims. The common thread among populists is their rejection of Islam, migrants, elites, and Europe as defined by the European Union. They are united by their defence of an

118

imaginary, supposedly homogeneous people, thought to share the same culture, customs and values. While all populists emphasize identity, they do not all share the same values. In fact, the spectrum is so broad that anticlerical secularists and practising Catholics are both able to find affinities with populists, who span the likes of Geert Wilders, champion of homosexual rights and the liberation values of the 1960s, which Muslims supposedly cannot assimilate; the Polish PiS, which defends Christian morals and is opposed to same-sex marriage; Marine Le Pen, who defends a secular line more than a Catholic one and does not want to turn back the tide of sexual liberation;[17] and Italy's homophobic and anti-feminist Matteo Salvini. The only point in common that they are left with is their opposition to Islam, which transcends their divergences over what a society without Islam should look like.

In any case, votes, polls and surveys show that the populist electoral surge has not been accompanied by a conservative backlash in terms of values. Demands involving sexual freedom, LGBT rights and feminism are constantly on the rise, to the point, as mentioned earlier, of creating a ratchet effect: there is no turning back. The #MeToo movement is not a trend; it is a turning point. Apart from in Poland, the vast majority of populists insist on a secular culture and do not challenge the achievements of the 1960s. They are not invested in the values of the Church, and readily attack the religious establishment when they find it too soft on immigration. For instance, in 2009 Salvini's Lega Nord party embarked on an all-out campaign against the archbishop of Milan, Dionigi Tettamanzi, who had criticized the forced evacuation of Roma camps.[18] And when Wojciech Polak, archbishop of Gniezno and primate of the Catholic Church of Poland, announced in October 2017 that he would suspend any priest who took part in an anti-refugee demonstration, it whipped up a storm of protest on populist websites.[19]

It should be pointed out that a segment of the French left, for the sake of secularism, also became involved in the battle against Islamization and ended up joining the anti-immigration coalition, as part of the Comité Laïcité République, and even the far right, as part of Riposte laïque.

If it is not a value system, what does Europe's Christian identity mean to populists? It seems mainly to manifest itself in the transformation of Christian religious symbols (the cross, steeples, nativity scenes, etc.) into cultural identity markers that are not associated with religious practice, accompanied by the public removal of signs associated with other religions, or even the expulsion of people wearing these signs.

It is obvious that Christianity, especially Catholicism,[20] has considerable importance in Europe's social and cultural landscape: from official holidays to the names of villages; from the crosses by roadsides and upon mountaintops, to the churches at the heart of villages and neighbourhoods; down to the so-called Christian names given at baptism. Populism empties these signs of their religious significance. Such evisceration of the spiritual from religious symbols can be implicit or explicit. It is implicit, for example, when populists view the defence of Christian places of worship as a mere matter of safeguarding heritage. Marine Le Pen, among others, included in her electoral manifesto the desire to 'promote our heritage and our culture: defence of our heritage will again be made a priority, whether it is historical monuments or rural heritage (churches and such).'[21] This is the only reference to Christianity in her party programme and it categorizes churches as historical monuments. In other words, their value lies in their stonework, not in the work of their ministry. Many populists defend churches against mosques, as long as they remain empty, or at least quiet.

In France the issue came to a head around nativity scenes, which some populist mayors want to display in their city halls. Secular organizations responded by filing complaints against these exhibits in the name of separation of church and state. The Church does not come to the mayors' defence, since the matter is not one of faith. When asked what he thought about the nativity scene controversies, André Vingt-Trois, the rather conservative archbishop of Paris, answered:

> It's hogwash! The issue has been widely exploited to political ends that have little to do with Christmas. And

why not the Candlemas crêpes? I don't believe they come under *laïcité*. The Conseil d'État settled the matter by appealing to circumstances and the cultural nature of nativity scenes... Christian presence in society does not boil down to a couple of figurines in the town hall![22]

Crucifixes have been subject to similar controversies. In April 2018, the interior minister for Bavaria mandated the display of crucifixes in government buildings as 'an expression of Bavaria's social and cultural identity' and 'an affirmation of our cultural and historical, as well as our spiritual values'. No reference was made to Christian values; only the identity and culture of a social group were at stake. The minister went so far as to deny the religious nature of the cross. Speaking to the *Süddeutsche Zeitung*, Cardinal Reinhard Marx, archbishop of Munich, condemned the minister's decision, warning that, 'if the cross is viewed only as a cultural symbol, then it has not been understood.' There indeed lies the crux of the matter. The issue is not only that of dissociating a cultural marker from a religious marker. Cultural significance now prevails over religious meaning, which was not the case when society's dominant culture was infused with religiosity.

For the Church, it is thus not merely an issue of folklorizing religious symbols (something it has always accepted in the context of popular devotion), but indeed a conflict between two sets of values, all the more since the rehabilitation of Christian symbols is explicitly presented, naturally at the expense of their religious significance, as the best way to get rid of Muslim symbols in public space. In 2009, Cardinal Christoph Schönborn, archbishop of Vienna, thus harshly reprimanded the Austrian populist Freedom Party (FPÖ) for using the cross on its anti-immigrant propaganda posters. The cardinal even affirmed that the Christian value that really came into play, far from rejecting the other, should be 'love thy enemy' (*Feindesliebe*).[23]

It is clear that the Church has a complex relationship to culture, or rather that its view of culture has changed. Local traditions were once a means of conveying faith. Consequently, from the blessing of animals to that of Harley Davidsons, the Church tolerated a healthy amount of folklore so as not to exclude forms of popular piety that are often deeply grounded in a local culture. Popular culture was infused with profound piety. But when society's dominant culture became secularized, and the society of the spectacle and consumerism took over and altered local cultures in order to integrate them into an economic, ideological or political logic, the Church gave up on its symbols and instead set out to salvage their original spirit and meaning. When, for instance, processions in honour of the Virgin Mary in southern Italy turn into a homage to the local mafia boss, the priest withdraws and the pope protests.[24] Even when a procession is quite innocent, the Church is now concerned that culture and identity could take precedence over the spiritual dimension.[25]

Seeing the return of Christian cultural symbols to public space as the starting point to win back souls is absurd. Those who promote it care little for the teachings of the Church; their intentions pertain more to folklore, entertainment, spectacle and exploitation. Paradoxically, bringing back Christian symbols actually helps to secularize religion.

The problem is that neither the populists nor even the Church are in control of religious symbols. Ultimately, it is the courts that decide, for if the Church considers that a religious marker is not religious enough, or no longer religious at all, secularists on the other hand believe that it is still too religious. Thus, secular normativity is actually what determines the meaning of religious symbols today.

8

The End of Christian Europe or the End of Religion?

Outside of communities of faith, religion is now widely perceived in Europe as a problem. As discussed, there are three discernible fronts in this battle. First, the hardcore secularists: for them, religion is in itself abominable, but their focus today is on the threat posed by Islam, rather than the Church. While this secular front views Salafism as their number one enemy, it is probably no more sympathetic toward processions of priests and altar boys dressed in white robes and bearing large wooden crosses, or to Orthodox Jews who sport their sidelocks in the streets of European capitals. Then there are the identitarians, for whom Christianity is bound up with Europe's identity, just as long as it does not interfere with their daily life, lecture them on loving their neighbour or preach to them about ethics and values. Last, there are, of course, faith communities who believe that their own religion (but not that of others) is part of the solution and not the problem. French bishops, for example, constantly praise French *laïcité*, and at one point even volunteered to teach Muslims the concept.[1]

Islam: An Accelerator of Religious Change in Europe

For the past thirty years or so, since the first 'Islamic headscarf' controversy in France erupted in 1989, Europe's relationship with Islam has dominated discussion of religion for two reasons. The first has to do with second-generation Muslim immigrants, who were themselves born in Europe. Many of them demand recognition of Islam in the public sphere, albeit in very different forms. The second is related to the advent of political Islam in the Middle East, starting with the Iranian Revolution of 1979 and followed by the rise of Islamist movements like the Muslim Brotherhood and the spread of 'globalized' terrorism via Al-Qaeda and Islamic State. Iran's Islamic Revolution left an impression on Western minds but had little impact on European Muslims, while the phenomenon of political and religious radicalization across the Sunni world has obviously had repercussions for what is now a globalized Islam.[2]

The aim here is not to discuss 'the Islamic question', on which there have been ample studies and discussions, but to examine the connections between the governance of Islam and the religious question in general. I remain convinced, however, as this book shows, that when it comes to the religious question, we are dealing with long-term trends that far predate the advent of the Islamic question.

There have been some recent controversies around religion in Europe that have no apparent relation to Islam; for instance, the issue over crucifixes in Italy. Yet, since religious issues are generally dealt with in 'crisis mode', they tend to be settled by parliaments and courts (ultimately by the European Court of Human Rights), under pressure from public opinion mobilized around specific cases. My hypothesis is that the governance of Islam by the courts amounts to reshaping the entire religious scene in Europe, and hence leads to rethinking Christianity, which has already been pushed to the sidelines by secularization and the Catholic Church's internal crisis. The question here is whether decisions made by the European Court and other tribunals are 'Islamophobic' or not (the term is too vague to be truly useful). The aim is to study their impact on Europe's relationship to Christianity. This impact is in fact negative for Christianity, because it denies the relevance of religion in general.

In fact, decisions concerning Islam all have consequences for Christianity, and even more for Judaism. Laws passed by parliaments and court decisions in European countries (backed by the European Court of Human Rights) largely fall into two categories. First, there are those that set more restrictive rules regarding religious practice in general, even if their primary objective is to set restrictions on Islam. These include restricting the conspicuous display of all religious symbols in parts of the public sphere, and placing bans on circumcision and ritual slaughter. Second, there are those that reinforce or affirm the primacy of a Christian identity that is essentially cultural (what the German courts have termed *Leitkultur*): the preservation of Christian symbols to the exclusion of all others in public spaces (in Italy and Bavaria), the minaret ban in Switzerland, and so on. But both these kinds of restrictive policies come up against a challenge: they are obliged to respect religious freedom. How can secularization and religious freedom be reconciled? How can the recognition of Christianity as the majority religion be made compatible with freedom for other religions?

Despite their diversity, all European constitutions concur de facto on a number of points concerning religion. They all recognize religious freedom, which does not only mean the right not to be discriminated against for one's 'identity' (as for race and gender) or simply to enjoy freedom of belief (as for a political or philosophical opinion), but which also includes the right to *practise* one's religion. The most restrictive law in Europe, France's 1905 Law on the Separation of Church and State, is very clear: it does not meddle in matters of religion (precisely because there is separation) or individual faith (which pertains to the private sphere), but concerns 'worship': in other words, religious practice. While it does place limits on religious practice, the Law of 1905 more importantly organizes how it manifests in the public sphere (buildings, processions, chaplaincies, religious symbols, bell ringing, praying in public, the freedom to practise, legal exemptions such as the seal of confession, etc.). In no way does it ban wearing religious symbols in public spaces; priests who have also been politicians, like Abbé Pierre and Canon Kir, both elected to public office well after 1905, were never prohibited from wearing the cassock in parliament (whereas for many years, female MPs were not allowed to wear trousers).

A clarification is needed here: parliaments and the courts have never expressly attested to the equality of religions, but have only prescribed limitations on freedom of religious practice (and freedom of expression). They may sometimes affirm the right to display the symbol of a particular religion (Christianity in this case) to the detriment of others if it corresponds to a 'culture'. Likewise, no religious community has asked for the equality of religions; they simply want respect for their own practices (keeping kosher, for instance) and beliefs (for Christians, the right to exemptions of conscience, for example over performing abortions or same-sex marriages, or to dismiss teachers in private Catholic schools who remarry after divorce).

In fact, respect for religious freedom does not necessarily imply equal treatment of religions. Some religions may be the official state religion (as in Denmark and the United Kingdom) or have special status (such as the automatic registry of Catholic marriages by the Italian civil registry, or the legal status of Christianity and Judaism as statutory corporations in Germany). But, in a departure from the state as conceived in the Treaty of Westphalia, no state today can impose a religion or interfere in theological debates. Nor can states defend any form of religious proselytism. In this regard, all states are neutral, including those under a concordat with the Holy See. This means that—contrary to what French ultra-secularists might believe—government officials may participate in religious events without it signifying support for that religion, but only as long as they do not endorse the dissemination of a religious message. States may use Christian symbols such as the cross, but it must purely be for cultural reasons and not with any intention to proselytize (the crosses on the British, Scandinavian and Swiss flags, for instance, do not have any kind of missionary message).

But the separation between the theological and the political works both ways. A French citizen cannot, in the name of the equality between men and women enshrined in her country's constitution, sue the Catholic Church for refusing to admit her to the seminary—at least not for the moment. These questions illustrate what is at stake, as we shall see.

The state cannot interfere in matters of theology, for instance, the interpretation of a verse in the Bible or the Qur'an, but only in the actions of people who might claim inspiration from it. Thus, no one can sacrifice his or her eldest son to God, claiming to have had a revelation, but

Revelations itself is granted immunity. The courts' only room for manoeuvre is in deciding whether the defence of religion (or indeed culture) is considered a mitigating or aggravating factor. My intuition (to be confirmed by research into jurisprudence) is that from the 1990s to the 2010s, there has been a shift from the former to the latter. In any event, this is clearly the case as regards female genital mutilation for the cultural sphere and circumcision for the religious.

The Courts' Expedition of Europe's Secularization

Here let us examine a number of landmark court cases over the past fifteen years, because they indicate broad trends in European law.

Laws on Religious Symbols

Some countries have passed laws to limit the wearing of Islamic dress. All over Europe, there has been a growing tendency to ban the burqa, which is never presented as the expression of a religious practice (mainly because it is a matter of personal choice and not a theological obligation). It has been banned primarily on security grounds and for reasons of 'living together', thereby eluding the religious question.

As regards the Muslim headscarf, its religious nature cannot be denied: many Muslim theologians consider it an obligation. Since the state cannot determine the correct interpretation of the Qur'an, it has to recognize that the hijab is indeed a religious symbol. This has given rise to two types of legislation: either only the hijab is considered to pose a problem, or the place of all religious signs is re-evaluated. France opted for the latter in 2004, when a law was passed banning all religious symbols in public schools. The question had not arisen previously. While Christian or Jewish symbols were rare, they were tolerated, and never clearly defined. The law on the headscarf does not address the equality of religions, but the question of religious signs in general.

Except that, all of a sudden, all religious symbols have been removed from certain public spaces in France: the Catholic chaplain's cassock (which had in fairness already virtually disappeared), the Jewish kippah, Sikh turbans— even, according to minister Luc Ferry, 'large Assyro-Chaldean crosses' (if such crosses ever existed in the first place).[3] The next stage in the secularization of the public sphere is indeed underway.

The second type of legal decision on the headscarf (in Germany and Switzerland) specifically bans the Islamic veil in official state buildings and refuses to extend this ban to Christian signs, arguing that Christianity is part of the dominant culture (*Leitkultur*). Here, the problem is posed differently: according to what principle can Christian symbols be protected?[4]

THE END OF CHRISTIAN EUROPE OR THE END OF RELIGION?

Circumcision

On 7 May 2012, in a case filed against a physician who had performed a circumcision on a child from a Muslim family, the district court in Cologne, Germany, found that male circumcision amounted to grievous bodily harm, even if performed by a doctor, unless it is carried out on medical grounds. Two arguments were put forward in justifying the decision: circumcision is: 1) a violation of a child's bodily integrity; and 2) a violation of his right to religious freedom, as it imposes on the child an irreversible religious mark that he has not been able to choose. The first argument engages with a classic conflict between competing rights: religious freedom and bodily integrity. But the second is more original and far more significant, because it sets the child's religious freedom against that of the parents: 'The body of the child is irreparably and permanently changed by a circumcision. This change contravenes the interests of the child to decide later on his religious beliefs.'[5]

Religious freedom is defined here as strictly individual: the child must be allowed to grow up without being indoctrinated by a religion, which should be only one option among others. Behind the defence of religious freedom lies a redefinition of what religion is—no longer either tradition or community, but a choice among other possibilities. Put simply, religious freedom can only be exercised in a secularized and religiously sterilized environment, so that a person's choice in adulthood is not subject to any pressure or constraint.

One can certainly denounce circumcision on the basis of the first argument. However, it must be recognized that the second argument deprives religion of having any divine and historical dimensions. It fails to affirm the state's neutrality in religious matters, instead instating relativism as an official doctrine. The Catholic Church was not mistaken: the cardinal-archbishop of Cologne, Joachim Meisner, said that the court decision was instituting a 'state duty to protect children against their parents' choices.'[6] Here again, we are back to a debate about the model of the family.

Following an outcry from the Jewish community, the decision was annulled by a law passed in the Bundestag (it must be remembered that one of the first decisions of the Nazi regime was to ban circumcision and ritual slaughter). This does not, however, render the original ruling irrelevant, since parliament did not contest the court's argumentation. It made a political rather than juridical decision by stating that Jewish and Muslim communities should be able to live in Germany. But in other countries that have not been subject to this political censure, campaigns against circumcision and ritual slaughter are in full swing. Iceland banned circumcision in 2018, and a ban is being seriously considered in Scandinavia.

Ritual Slaughter

On 17 February 2018, Denmark banned (or watered down, according to the official version) the process of ritual slaughter for kosher or halal meat. The argument used is one of animal suffering, initiating a classic conflict of rights, in which regard the Danish minister for agriculture, Dan Jorgensen, is said to have claimed that 'animal welfare comes before religion'.[7] This should not be seen merely as a subtle expression of anti-Semitism or Islamophobia (even though that is the motivation of some advocates of the ban). The animal rights movement is spreading across Europe, and becoming increasingly radical, today attacking halal and non-halal butchers alike, as well as pharmaceutical laboratories, hunters, furriers, and meat-eaters in general.

Here again, a critical anthropological change is looming. The hierarchy of natural rights is being called into question by collapsing the distinction between man and animal that has been clearly established throughout Christian and Western tradition. The God of Genesis creates animals before man, but twice he instructs Adam and Eve to rule over them.[8] Descartes held that man and animal are differentiated by man's ability to think—*cogito*. Modern anthropology has defined culture as arising out of a disconnection from nature.

The dissolution of this boundary goes hand in hand with the growing use of ethology (the study of animal social behaviour) and evolution to justify human practices, from monogamy to polygamy and even to rape, thus dispensing with a debate on values. It also coincides with artificial intelligence research, which works to create autonomous beings capable of reason, seen as independent from humans.

'Man is neither angel nor beast,' said Pascal. Today his hierarchy is falling apart, as humans lose their place between the dignified animal and the cold angel of algorithms. The disintegration of this natural pecking order is another extension of secularization.

Blasphemy

Both Islamic and Christian organizations have attempted to ban works on the grounds of 'blasphemy'. The notion of blasphemy, or offence against God, sets out two different orders: the sacred and the profane. (It is not possible to blaspheme the profane by definition, but only to insult or mock.) Since they do not accept this hierarchy, legislation in secular countries cannot endorse the notion of blasphemy. Following the case of *The Satanic Verses*, a novel by Salman Rushdie published in 1988, which led to violent demonstrations and a fatwa sentencing Rushdie to death, the few European countries that still had laws prohibiting blasphemy—even if, as in the UK, they had fallen into disuse—hastened to repeal the articles in question.

Oddly enough there have been recent cases, including in ultra-secular France, in which the courts have become involved. The most interesting case, which was not struck down by the Court of Cassation because no appeal was made, is of the complaint filed by a Catholic organisation against the fashion company Marithé et François Girbaud in 2005. The facts are straightforward: an advertising campaign for the clothing brand put up posters in Paris streets with a scene that parodied Leonardo da Vinci's painting *The Last Supper* (1498), replacing Christ's apostles with scantily clad young women. The court condemned the ad on the following grounds:

> The decision to display this imposing poster in places of public passage is *a gratuitous and aggressive act of intrusion on people's innermost beliefs.…* The scene's levity moreover does away with the whole tragic nature that is nevertheless inherent in the first event of the Passion.… The offence done to Catholics far outweighs the desired commercial goal.

Two remarks are in order. First, the court did not say that the poster parodied da Vinci (which is obviously the case, given that the painting is far better known than the passage in the Gospel of Luke), but rather that it parodied Jesus and the apostles. By ignoring that Leonardo da Vinci is a great artist and his work belongs to everyone, not to the Church, there is thus an implicit denial of the painting's cultural dimension. The Church more or less saw fit to grant itself copyright on the Last Supper, in other words, on any representation of the institution of the Eucharist, because it is essential dogma. Thus the very concept of Christian culture is denied, in the rejection of the idea that an element of religious origin can be shifted to a profane cultural context where believers and non-believers alike can enjoy it without being required to show their baptismal certificate. This has the effect of entrenching the disconnect between religious marker and cultural marker, since it removes the possibility of being both at once. In short, the courts serve to ratify, or at least bear witness to, the deculturation of the religious sphere.

But the second dimension is even more interesting. The court did not penalize offence to the sacred, that is, to Christ (whom it cannot consider a subject of law any more than Prophet Muhammad), but to the suffering inflicted on religious men and women. The matter is no longer one of blasphemy, but of damages. By penalizing the offence to believers, the court secularizes the sacred dimension; we are no longer talking about transgression against the sacred, but about damages awarded for the suffering of individuals. In keeping with the values of the 1960s, this suffering is deemed unacceptable, since the individual has the right to happiness, inner peace, and to simply be left alone. It is a far cry from the Gospel's vivid sense of the tragic. Thus, in this sort of judgment, the court secularizes the soul itself.

The Revocation of Clerical Immunity

Faith communities of all religious persuasions are no longer able to impose their 'non-negotiable moral issues' on society.

Consequently, they fall back on claiming exemptions for reasons of conscience, which would allow them not to have to comply with certain statutory obligations that go against their beliefs. These matters are decided by the courts on a case-by-case basis, but on the whole, secularism is making inroads. Even in the US, while the Supreme Court sided with a Colorado baker who refused to make a wedding cake for a gay couple, state employees are denied the right to refrain from issuing licences for same-sex marriages.

The Church's protection of paedophile priests and its ensuing obstruction of investigations have had devastating effects for its authority. Not only have its reputation and image been ruined (how can it lecture on abortion and the sanctity of life when it covers up child abuse?), but the scandals have also prompted the public and the authorities to challenge entire aspects of the religious sphere. The clearest example of this is in Australia, where in June 2018 the ACT Legislative Assembly passed laws requiring priests to break the seal of confession in cases concerning child abuse. The measure is sensible in view of the Church's reluctance to report guilty priests. But, as pointed out by the archbishop of Canberra, Christopher Prowse, it is also 'an intrusion in the sacramental life of the Church,'[9] as confession is a condition of receiving the Eucharist and therefore of salvation. If the sinner does not confess for fear of being reported, then the very purpose of the Church, assuring the salvation of souls, is put in jeopardy. Some might say that the ban only pertains to cases of sexual abuse, but given the rising demand for transparency in our societies, the list of crimes and misdemeanours revoking the seal of confession will surely grow longer, until only those whose sin is masturbation will have hope of eternal salvation.

If, in this instance, the Church only has itself to blame, the outcome is in line with my hypothesis concerning the extension of secularization and dechristianization in the West. In the case of confession, the secular powers refuse to take into account the theological question, which is in keeping with their role. But there are more and more situations in which public opinion, mostly dechristianized, is demanding that the secular powers intervene in theology. In 2009, in Recife, Brazil, a nine-year-old girl, who had been raped by her stepfather and was pregnant with twins, underwent an abortion for medical reasons. The archbishop of Recife, José Cardoso Sobrinho (who had been appointed by John Paul II in 1985 to replace the progressive bishop Dom Hélder Câmara) excommunicated both the girl's mother and the physician, but later withdrew his pronouncement for the mother because (under pressure from the parish priest) she claimed to have changed her mind about having consented to the abortion. The public was outraged, all the more since the rapist was not excommunicated. The archbishop then explained that according to canon law, abortion, which for the Church amounts to murder, is far more serious than rape. This pronouncement caused a furore. Many in the Church denounced the bishop's lack of compassion, but did so without calling into question the hierarchy of sins he had outlined according to canon law. Two diametrically opposed worlds have thus emerged in terms of values. Public debate over abortion is perfectly normal, but debate over excommunication is far more surprising: why would non-believers feel concerned about the salvation of someone's soul? Why not simply condemn the Church's attitude to abortion? Why demand it make amends for its theology if one is not a member? Why demand the Eucharist for all?

Such interference of the secular in theology affects all religions. Among practising Jews, *halakha* stipulates that a woman seeking divorce must receive written permission from her husband, the *get* document, without which she is not authorized to remarry. Civil courts should not concern themselves with this, and yet, even in France, they sometimes do so on the grounds of moral harm. At the same time as recognizing the weight of religion, this approach also 'tames' and psychologizes it, working from the presumption that belief itself amounts to suffering damage.[10] As for Islam, a petition in France recently called for certain verses to be struck from the Qur'an, of course without demanding the removal of very similar verses in the books of Exodus or Leviticus.[11] But even if the petitioners had done so, the problem remains the same: demanding that a sacred text be corrected is to affirm the relativity of any

141

religious revelation. It undermines religious truth itself; it secularizes it. Dictating that religious norms align with secular norms is problematic in a liberal democracy, because it denies the fact that religion is religious (the Chinese government, which applies this principle across the board for its Muslims and Catholics, does not have such a problem).

Bureaucratic Regulation

Another, more discreet dimension of secularization has to do with regulation, and unfolds especially in countries that have a strong secular tradition. In France, for example, the 2004 law banning conspicuous religious symbols in school has been interpreted with excessive zeal, with skirts that are deemed too long and bandanas[12] being treated as religious signs (beards have escaped the ban because hipsters give them secular credentials). Almost everything is at risk of being seen as religious. The burkini, which is found nowhere in the Qur'an or in the Prophet's *hadith*, or even on the beaches of Saudi Arabia, is treated as a religious sign, as is the fact of not eating meat in school canteens. Obsession with religion leads to seeing religion everywhere, resulting in overzealous regulations.

An interesting example can be found in French prisons. The Law of 1905 on the Separation of Church and State obliges the state to appoint prison chaplains. When in the first decade of the new millennium it became clear that prisons had become a hotbed of Islamic radicalization, the penitentiary administration agreed to introduce Muslim chaplains. But, like all other chaplains, they were not allowed to contact prisoners on their own initiative, out of fear that the chaplains would proselytize. This makes little sense, since the point of calling on the services of Muslim chaplains in the first place was to provide an alternative to the conversion of prisoners to Salafism. The result is that, in the name of *laïcité*, and out of fear of proselytism, the chaplain is supposed to wait in his office for a detainee to make a written request to meet with him, which of course only happens very rarely. Meanwhile, radical Islam proliferates in prisons, spread by the prisoners themselves.

Intensity of religious practice is considered a sign of radicalization, as is evident in the guidance for spotting radical behaviour published by the French government in February 2018.[13] On the other hand, transgression of religious norms is viewed as a sign of moderation: 'He's a Muslim, but he drinks alcohol' is often used as an argument to prove that a job applicant is not a 'radical'. Many Muslims apply to be baggage handlers at Charles-de-Gaulle airport, given the airport's proximity to Seine-Saint-Denis which has large Arab and Sub-Saharan African communities, and so when the police conduct an investigation to approve their security clearance, one of the first questions has to do with religious practice. The best way to get through the interview without difficulty is to spontaneously mention drinking alcohol: one of the rare instances in which drinking makes it easier to get a job.

All these cases show how secularism is eradicating even the slightest sign of religiosity from the public arena, how it contributes to emptying the public space of all spirituality, but also relegates religion not to the private sphere (to which it does not belong, by definition), but to the margins, where it can fall easily into the hands of radicals.

The Defence of Christian Identity: A Contribution to Secularization

In some instances, the courts have been called on to determine whether a case should be made for Christian exceptionalism. This would not only confirm that the principle of religious freedom does not imply equality of religions, but it would also assert Christianity as an integral part of Europe's dominant culture, meaning that its presence in the public sphere would be a matter of course, regardless of the faith and religious practice of Europeans.

It is obvious that there is inequality today between religions in Europe, but this also reflects history, past culture and demography. Muslim authorities usually follow the model of Jewish communities, which have embraced their minority status. No believer is demanding that a crescent or star of David be added alongside every cross in public view, or that public holidays be granted for every religious festival, or that Christian places be renamed[14] (unlike anti-racists, who argue for name changes as part of the 'decolonization' of buildings and public spaces). Demands for equality come instead from multiculturalist circles, which are the democratic equivalent of populist identitarians.[15] Both groups see religious signs as cultural markers, which is why the former insist on equality among symbols and the latter on the supremacy of Christian symbols. It is a deeply secular demand in that it grants equal importance to everything within the religious sphere, thus dismissing the standpoint of believers of all persuasions, for whom religious symbols have to do with transcendence rather than immanence, and sacredness rather than mundaneness. Examination of jurisprudence and decisions by the European Court of Human Rights, however, shows that every time the Court defends unequal treatment of religions in favour of Christianity, it always does so by reducing the Christian sign to a purely cultural marker.

The Muslim Veil and the Nun's Veil

In the case of Fereshta Ludin, a female teacher who was denied a job in Stuttgart in 1998 because she wore a headscarf, at the end of intricate judicial proceedings, the parliament in Baden-Württemberg passed a law mandating political and religious neutrality for teachers, but made exceptions for 'Christian or other traditional Western beliefs'.[16] A teaching nun could therefore wear her veil, but a Muslim teacher had to remove her headscarf. The German Federal Constitutional Court ultimately overturned this jurisprudence, but the parliament's reasoning is still often used to set limitations only on Islam, as a 'foreign' religion. The problem, as discussed, is that Christian values and Western values no longer coincide. This explains the very vague reference to 'cultural' traditions, as if Christian values were defined only as cultural markers.

Minarets in Switzerland

In November 2009, the Swiss government passed a law prohibiting the building of minarets following the results of a referendum vote. The case will undoubtedly reach the European Court of Human Rights sooner or later. As the Swiss constitution guarantees religious freedom, the only way to prohibit minarets is to make them out to be cultural and non-essential to the rites of worship. For once this is actually the case: minarets, which did not exist in Muhammad's time, were originally inspired by church steeples. They are in no way an essential aspect of religious observance. All ritual requirements of the religion can be met without a minaret, and mosques without minarets are not affected by the ban, so there is no violation of religious freedom. The ban on minarets as 'cultural' objects is justified on the grounds that they conflict with Swiss architecture and landscape, aspects of Swiss culture. The argument of the Swiss state helps to deculturalize Islam and thus paradoxically makes it more compatible with Europe. Turkish mosques can no longer be built in Switzerland, but nothing prohibits the construction of Swiss mosques (with a clock tower, for instance). The other consequence is that Islam is contrasted not with Christianity as a religion, but with a Western cultural aesthetic, which, as we have seen, is in many aspects contrary to Christian norms. Yodelling instead of the call to prayer: how kitsch can you get? Once again, Christianity is secularized to combat Islam.

The Case of the Crucifix[17]

In 1950s Italy, the political and social situation was extremely polarized, as it was in France, with a strong communist party, a Christian democrat party and two respective civil societies. Crucifixes could be seen hanging in many classrooms. No communist elected official had ever asked for their removal. It took a Finnish atheist worried about the harmful influence of the crucifix on her son for the case to wind up before the European Court of Human Rights in 2009. The argument was that the presence of the crucifix was in itself a form of proselytism. To justify the presence of the crucifix, attorneys for the Italian government defined it as simply a national symbol of Italian culture, arguing that it could not be construed as representing proselytism since it had nothing to do with faith. In the eyes of the Italian government, the crucifix has basically become a cultural piece of wood. The state won, but the bishops were rightfully concerned that a religious symbol could thus be likened to a cultural prop.[18] Once again, the crucifix cause was won but religion was secularized in the process. Thus, either culture is favoured and religion is sacrificed, or religion takes primacy and culture becomes irrelevant. As in the case of nativity scenes in France,[19] the transformation of the crucifix into a cultural object means that we are no longer talking about religion.

Religion and the European Court of Human Rights

In the above overview of European Court decisions, it is obvious that in cases involving religious issues, the Court overwhelmingly applies the principle of subsidiarity, that is, allowing states to handle all matters that they are able to manage without the assistance of a higher authority at the European level. Consequently, France can ban the burqa—a law that, according to the Court, constitutes a violation of religious freedom—because the concept of 'living together' is an element of French culture, as is *laïcité*.

A religion, in this case Christianity, can only have primacy if it corresponds to the dominant culture (*Leitkultur*). Thus, the Court has ratified religion as an aspect of the national culture and refrained from giving religious freedom a general definition. Both the ban on the burqa in France and toleration of the crucifix in Italy are justified on the grounds of 'national culture': the French are secularists and the Italians are Catholics. In the name of the principle of subsidiarity,[20] the Court not only rejects the idea that Europe is Christian but also refuses the idea of a dominant religious culture in Europe by ascribing both religion and secularism to national cultures. By reducing religion to culture, it secularizes it.

The European Court decision of 23 October 2018 (*E.S. v. Austria*), upholding the Austrian court's conviction of a woman who had called Prophet Muhammad a 'paedophile', sums up the Court's perspective. The ECHR gave three arguments in line with the examples given here: 1) according to the subsidiarity principle, every country has the right to have its own legislation regarding religion, an argument that thereby upholds political control over the religious sphere; 2) it is the state's duty to ensure social harmony and the peaceful coexistence among groups, and consequently to control 'hate speech'; 3) the accusation made by the defendant offended believers' religious feelings.

Far from reviving the crime of blasphemy (which it explicitly rejected), the Court deliberately ignored the sacred dimension of religion; it even reduced faith to a 'feeling' and the faith community to a category of individuals identified by any trait: race, gender or religion. It thus secularizes the religious sphere by placing it with other profane categories and, in keeping with the Treaty of Westphalia, entrusts the governance of this sphere to secular states.

If Christianity's place in society is shrinking, it is because, in addition to the broad trend of secularization, the urge to limit the role of Islam amounts to reducing the religious sphere in general. At the same time, the desire to promote

Christian identity as a means to counter the rise of Islam results in the increased secularization of Christianity.

Secularists are helping to undo the link between Europe and Christianity, which explains their shift toward identity politics. But it is very odd to see observant Christian intellectuals cling to an identitarian Christianity that eviscerates the very spirituality they claim to cultivate in their hearts.

The only thing that could invalidate the thesis developed here and that could possibly justify the position of identitarian believers would be an overwhelming return to faith and Christian religious practice, as a result of the activism of the remaining Catholics. But to pass laws and impose religious symbols, to take up Pascal's wager of pretending to believe because there is nothing to lose and everything to gain by waiting for the intervention of Providence and the Holy Spirit, is no guarantee of success. Strangely, these intellectuals, from Rod Dreher to Rémi Brague and Pierre Manent, are deeply pessimistic, because they are essentialists; they confuse culture with religion, and cannot see that both are in crisis, or at least evolving. Perhaps while waiting for the Holy Spirit, it would be better to recover the unbearable lightness of being. If Europe is to become Christian again, it is in need of prophets, not legislators. But the prophets may very well turn out not to be where one expects to find them.

Conclusion

Values are returning today in the guise of dominant norms, both in the secular world and in religion. Today's crisis is not simply a crisis of values, but of referring to values at all. For what should values be founded on?

On one hand, religions, which are no longer in sync with Europe's dominant cultures, are returning to the public sphere on behalf of a normative demand. Catholics and evangelicals alike battle over the letter of the law, to restrict or prohibit the right to abortion, same-sex marriage or relaxation of the rules of procreation. They claim to preach transcendent morality, but their ambivalence with regard to populists and identitarians, their withdrawal from other major societal issues, and their siege mentality make their message inaudible.

If secularization is the devil, then the devil is everywhere, and it has even managed to don the guise of religion, for secularization is at the very heart of religious processes today. In cases of conflicting normativity, it is always secularism that wins out, because religion cannot prove or legitimate its values any other way than by setting an example, and in this the Church can hardly be said to be shining like a beacon on a hill.

On the other hand, the secular culture that professes freedom and rights is coming to a head in a burst of normative production. This is a normativity toward all forms of religion and religiosity, of course, but also normativity with respect to its own foundation, the social contract (for many no longer wish to adhere to it) and human nature, that of the desiring subject. For if all cultures are patriarchal, it must be because there is a patriarchal constant that cannot be eradicated by culture, which, in this case, has been unable to perceive its own violence. The problem of patriarchy must therefore be rectified by the establishment of a moral norm, hence secularism's recourse to the law. However, the state does not itself produce values; it only produces norms and laws, and thus the truth is now handed down by the courts instead of the Church.

Social contract theory, at the foundation of liberal societies, is faltering, because it is unable to respond to the paradox stated by the German legal scholar Ernst-Wolfgang Böckenförde (himself a Catholic intellectual): 'The liberal secular state lives on premises that it is not able to guarantee,'[1] for then it would cease to be liberal. A liberal society can only function on a consensus, whether cultural or based on the social contract. But where in the war of values can this consensus be found?

'Culture' is in crisis; ideologies, religions, and communication systems can only travel around the world if they are first stripped of elements of local culture. The social contract has ceased to function, as liberal society contains antagonistic groups that take non-negotiable moral issues as their starting point, as matters that are not subject to debate. Charles Taylor did his best to justify the theory of 'reasonable accommodation', which consists of telling secularists to leave religion alone as long as it does not interfere with their freedom. A typical example was in Montreal, where a Hasidic Jewish community wanted to construct an *eruv*, erecting barely visible white strings three metres above their neighbourhood area to comply with rules of the Sabbath. The local council refused this arrangement on the grounds of secularism. As the examples given in his book show, contemporary secularism does not want to make any concessions to religion, even at the margins.

If consensus cannot come from the social contract, it can still be built around the tautology of identity: 'I am what I am, we are us.' The argument of identity provokes narcissistic ecstasy among populists, but the tautology is devoid of content, because any discussion or debate would immediately bring differences to the fore. The only way to lend substance to this sort of identity is through mimicry. French identitarians have organized get-togethers for indulging in pork sausages and red wine in the streets. It is quite obvious who is being left out, who the 'other' is; it is by contrasting themselves with Jews and Muslims that these identitarians call themselves 'Christians'. The sausages and red wine are essentially caricatures of the Eucharist, metaphors that destroy what is being mimicked, in other words the Christianity that they supposedly promote.

Three registers organize the debate: secular normativity, religious normativity and identity, which mimics one and then the other in turn. If these registers should falter or fail, where will we be headed?

It is time to re-examine the question of values, to restore the particular cultural and social aspects of norms and to reinject them into society. In the face of globalization, the issue is at once to be more in touch with society and to act as a counterweight to other influences in the world: only Europe can meet these two objectives. We have no choice but to go back to fundamentals, in particular to those of European liberalism as well as what remains of its Christian heritage. We must go back to the foundations of the initial European project, beyond its bureaucratic systems. Ultimately, Europe is the only entity in which it remains possible to instil some spirit.

Notes

INTRODUCTION

1. https://www.timesofisrael.com/new-minister-raises-ire-by-saying-islam-not-part-of-germany

1. EUROPE'S CHRISTIAN HERITAGE

1. Such cultural turning points were the focus of the twentieth-century Annales school of French historians in their development of 'the history of mentalities'.

2. When speaking in general terms, 'secularists' is used in this book to talk about Europeans whose thinking and lifestyle are completely secularized, without their necessarily taking an anti-religious stance in the manner of the French *laïcité*, a guiding principle of the French state. 'French secularists' is used to mean those individuals who are staunchly opposed to any sign of religion in the public sphere. The French term '*laïcité*' is used in discussing the issue of state secularism in France.

3. Denis Crouzet, *Charles Quint. Empereur d'une fin des temps*, Paris: Odile Jacob, 2016.

4. Olivier Christin, *La Paix de religion. L'autonomisation de la raison politique au XVIᵉ siècle*, Paris: Seuil, 1997.

155

5. See Harold Berman, *Law and Revolution*, II: *The Impact of the Protestant Reformations on the Western Legal Tradition*, London: Belknap, 2006.
6. Maximilien Robespierre, *Discours sur la religion, la République, l'esclavage*, La Tour d'Aigues: Édition de l'Aube, 2016. The French Revolution was never secular. It wanted to absorb the religious sphere. It fought against the Church, not against religion.
7. Mark A. Noll, *The Scandal of the Evangelical Mind*, Grand Rapids: Eerdmans, 1995.
8. The American Civil War demonstrated the limits of federalism too.
9. In October 2017, Crown Prince Mohammed bin Salman had a dozen Wahhabi clerics arrested, accusing them of hostility toward the government's religious law reforms.
10. Luther never took an interest in such endeavours and the Protestant missions began much later, in the early nineteenth century.
11. Philip Jenkins, *Next Christendom: The Coming of Global Christianity*, New York: Oxford University Press, 2011.
12. See the Salon Beige website: https://www.lesalonbeige.fr

2. DOES SECULARIZATION MEAN DECHRISTIANIZATION?

1. Jean Baubérot, *Les Laïcités dans le monde*, Paris: Presses Universitaires de France, 2014.
2. See works by Michel Vovelle, Pierre Chaunu and Philippe Haudrère.
3. See works by Kaspar von Greyerz, Jean Delumeau, and Louis Pérouas on the La Rochelle diocese, Pierre Chaunu and, more recently, Guillaume Cuchet.
4. See works by Gabriel Le Bras, Canon Fernand Boulard and others.

5. http://geoconfluences.ens-lyon.fr/actualites/veille/breves/
    pratique-religieuse-france

6. Pew Research Center, *Being Christian in Western Europe*,
    29 May 2018.

7. https://www.stmarys.ac.uk/research/centres/benedict-xvi/
    docs/2017-may-no-religion-report.pdf

8. Guillaume Cuchet, *Comment notre monde a cessé d'être
    chrétien. Anatomie d'un effondrement*, Paris: Seuil, 2018.

9. https://www.eleves.ens.fr/aumonerie/en_ligne/toussaint04/
    seneve004.html

10. Translated by Jean Lerner as *The Vanishing Peasant: Innovation
    and Change in French Agriculture*, Cambridge, MA: The MIT
    Press, 1971.

11. http://books.openedition.org/puc/121?lang=

12. On the matter of ties between regional nationalism and
    Catholicism, see Xabier Itçaina's seminal research on the Basque
    Country: *Catholic Mediations in Southern Europe: The Invisible
    Politics of Religion*, Abingdon and New York: Routledge, 2019.

13. Józef Baniak, 'Powołania do kapłaństwa i życia zakonnego w
    Polsce w latach 1900-2010', *Studium Socjologiczne*, Poznań
    UAM, 2012, as well as the *Annuarium Statisticum Ecclesiae in
    Polonia AD 2018*, Instytut Statystyki Kościoła Katolickiego,
    Warsaw, 2018.

14. Pew Research Center poll, *Being Christian in Western Europe*,
    29 May 2018.

15. Sofres poll, 'Les Français et la religion', https://www.tns-sofres.
    com/sites/default/files/050407_religion.pdf

16. https://www.kristeligt-dagblad.dk/kirke-tro/
    hver-fjerde-dansker-tror-p%C3%A5-jesus

17. http://cle.ens-lyon.fr/espagnol/civilisation/histoire-espagnole/
    societe-contemporaine/la-laicite-en-espagne-un-compromis-
    hesitant-issu-de-memoires-conflictuelles#section-9

18. https://www.catholicnewsagency.com/news/number-of-
    german-priest-ordinations-plummets-to-new-low-96548

19. A parish priest in Aubagne told me that he had to intervene (politely) in a marriage celebration because they had planned to distribute six-packs of beer during the ceremony, of course thinking it harmless. Indifference and ignorance have replaced anticlericalism.

20. See Chapter 3.

3. ANOTHER SOURCE OF MORALITY? THE CHURCH VERSUS MODERNISM (1864–1964)

1. 'A society must want to be, in order to be.' Marcel Gauchet, *The Disenchantment of the World: A Political History of Religion*, trans. Oscar Burge, Princeton, NJ: Princeton University Press, 1999 [1985], p. 175.

2. The Republicans, who won the elections in 1877, were strongly anti-clerical and vowed to curb the influence of the Catholic Church.

3. Pope Benedict XIII, encyclical letter *Testem benevolentiæ*, 1899.

4. This compromise was reached in 1924, when Pope Pius XI issued the encyclical *Maximam gravissimamque*, endorsing bishops' control over parish priests.

5. In the interim, however, in 1910, Pope Pius X condemned the French Sillon movement, founded by Marc Sangnier. The movement was perceived by the Church as too modernist and republican.

6. Pope Pius XII's timid stance toward Nazism also contributed to undermining the Church's credibility as regards what was 'good' in politics, even if his predecessor, Pius XI, had openly condemned Nazism (in the encyclical *Mit Brennender Sorge*).

7. Given these doctrinal disputes, in 1998, John Paul II reinstated the 'profession of faith and oath of fidelity' (apostolic letter *Ad tuendam fidem*), 'which must be made by specific members of the faithful when they receive an office'.

4. THE SELF-SECULARIZATION OF RELIGION

1. Worker-priests were priests who decided to enrol as factory workers to reach out to the working class.

2. See below.

3. To understand the originality of Bonhoeffer's position, it is worth comparing it to that of the great theologian Karl Barth, who also opposed Hitler with his 'Confessing Church' and was the principal author of the famous Declaration of Barmen (1934) against 'German Christians' who backed the Führer. According to Barth, the absolute, transcendent nature of God should prevent a Christian from adhering to the Nazi idolatry of race, cults of personality, etc. (Bonhoeffer also signed the Barmen Declaration.)

4. This is clear in the liturgy for the dead: the hymn *Dies irae dies illa*, whose grandiose and frightening images had struck generations of Catholics, vanished from the funeral mass. The celebration now almost exclusively emphasizes the idea that the deceased 'rest in peace'.

5. Canon Dangoisse, who made a precise list of the changes in the new translation following the Council, gives the example of the phrasing of the missal 'Pray, brothers, that my sacrifice and yours may be acceptable to God the Almighty Father', which was replaced in French by 'Pray, brothers and sisters, … for our good and the good of all his holy Church' (*Les Mots de la messe. Propositions pour la révision des traductions du missel romain publié en 1970 par Paul VI*, Paris:Ad Solem, 2010). See also Yves Lambert, *Dieu change en Bretagne*, Paris: Cerf, 1985.

6. 'Let us pray for the perfidious Jews': disputes over this literal translation of the Latin word *perfidus* did not prevent it from being removed from the French and English version of the Good Friday mass. The call for Jews to convert was also removed. The word *perfidis* was removed in the Latin version too, although the Latin rite continues to call for Jews' conversion.

7.   *Gaudium et Spes*, Pastoral Constitution on the Church in the Modern World, especially paragraph 36. 'Autonomy' legitimates the independence of scientific research, for instance, but within the limits of 'natural identified law', laws that govern the world created by God. But the extension of autonomy, which promotes human freedom, has since become the rule for many Catholics.

8.   See the front page of *Libération* newspaper on the Synod on the Family in 2016, and the *Monde* poll on priestly celibacy on 21 September 2018.

5. THE TURNING POINT OF THE 1960S

1.   Subject to a complete inventory, not all these movements led to a transformation in the dominant values of society. The Chinese Cultural Revolution was somewhat puritanical (which put Western Maoists in a contradictory position regarding sexuality). It is therefore important to distinguish between the political and societal dimension of youth uprisings; the latter dimension only applies to the West.

2.   According to Danish law, for instance, the mother can be ordered to pay a fine if she refuses to divulge the identity of the putative father. Anders Eriksson and Akke Salden, 'Establishing and contesting parentage', in John Eekelaar, *Parenthood in Modern Society: Legal and Social Issues for the Twenty-First Century*, Le iden: Martinus Nijhoff Publishers, 1993, p. 82.

3.   See the many articles in *Libération* in the 1970s, the success of David Hamilton's erotic photos, or even Louis Malle's film *La Petite* (1978).

4.   *Valeurs Actuelles*, 23 October 2017.

6. THE RELIGIOUS SECESSION: THE ENCYCLICAL HUMANÆ VITÆ (JULY 1968)

1.   Benedict XVI's Address to Members of the European People's Party, 30 March 2006.

2.   In his homily during a mass in memory of Father Hamel, murdered in July 2016, attended by the French president, Cardinal Vingt-Trois denounced the 'silence of parents in front of their children and the breakdown in the transmission of common values', as well as 'the silence of elites before the deviance of mores and the legalization of these deviances'.

3.   'I therefore believe that throughout Europe, … we should give serious thought as to how to achieve a true evangelization in this day and age, not only a new evangelization, but often a true and proper first evangelization. People do not know God; they do not know Christ. There is a new form of paganism and it is not enough for us to strive to preserve the existing flock, although this is very important.' Address of Benedict XVI to German bishops, Cologne, Archbishop's House, on the occasion of the twentieth World Youth Day, Sunday, 21 August 2005. Regarding the dilution of Christian faith into a vague identity, see the statement made by a bishop to Benedict XVI: 'It is clear,' Cardinal Bagnasco said, 'that there is an attempt to dilute faith in order to extinguish it in the collective and personal conscience, reducing faith from a guiding force to a vague memory', http://www.mondayvatican. com/vatican/a-warning-by-cardinal-bagnasco-and-benedict-xvis-former-students

4.   The expression 'culture of death' appears twelve times in Pope John Paul II's 1995 encyclical *Evangelium vitæ* on 'the value and inviolability of human life'.

5.   A cartoon by Plantu in *Le Monde* newspaper in the 1980s shows a traditional family in front of the television. When it is announced that the pope is about to address the audience, the mother tells her husband, 'Quick, put the children to bed. He's going to talk about sex again!'

6.   I studied this phenomenon in *Holy Ignorance: When Religion and Culture Part Ways* (trans. Ros Schwarz), London/New York: Hurst/Columbia University Press, 2010.

7. See Chapter 7.
8. The label 'fundamentalist' mainly applies to the Society of Saint Pius X, founded by Marcel Lefebvre in Écône, Switzerland, in the 1970s. It was deemed heretical in 1988 when Archbishop Lefebvre ordained bishops without approval from the Holy See.
9. In the community or the parish assembly, this also implies a return to practical positions of power and authority over the laity.
10. Insistence on 'adoration' and kneeling during consecration, and reversion to the Host given on the tongue and not in the hand. In general, the success of 'adoration' of the consecrated Host, a typical practice of Catholic devotion that declined after Vatican II, shows the strength of the comeback of traditional (now traditionalist) spirituality, which has a tendency to 'sanctify' the worship service, the objects of worship and its ministers (the priest).
11. See 'France; à propos des catholiques tradismatiques', Religioscope website, 17 January 2017, https://www.religion. info/2017/01/17/france-catholiques-tradismatiques
12. The book by the leader of Communion and Liberation, Julian Carron, *Dov'è Dio?* (Milan: Piemme, 2017), provides a good introduction to this spiritualist revival that takes into account the fact of secularized society.
13. Mario Giro, one of the community leaders, was a trade-unionist, undersecretary of state and then deputy minister for foreign affairs and international cooperation in the Renzi government (2013–2016). Sant'Egidio is a specific case: originally part of the charismatic tendency, which continues to have a strong influence on the community's spiritual life, the group is very involved in its relationship with the secular world and other religions. Sant'Egidio also serves parish churches and is very active in local charity work.
14. These communities have been established as institutions of pontifical right, either as 'faith communities', like the

Emmanuel, and Communion and Liberation, or as 'communities of clerics', such as the Community of Saint Martin.

15. See Mark A. Noll, *The Scandal of the Evangelical Mind*, op. cit., p. 60 ff.

16. This Protestantization of Catholic revivalism is very paradoxical, because the traditionalist Catholics' main criticism of Vatican II is that it set in motion (or sanctioned) a Protestantization of the Church.

17. In the Catholic Church, married deacons can perform certain priestly functions (give certain sacraments or witness them, preach, etc.). As 'ordained ministers', for the Church they are on the side of priests or the 'clergy', but as married people they are more perceived from the outside as 'laity'.

18. See Jean-Louis Schlegel's conclusion in Denis Pelletier and Jean-Louis Schlegel (eds), *À la gauche du Christ. Les chrétiens de gauche en France de 1945 à nos jours*, Paris: Seuil, 2012. Significantly, particularly in the massive crisis caused by revelations of paedophilia, they insist on the place of women in the Catholic Church, which is still unrecognized or only recognized in secondary roles without any real power.

19. Details can be found in the essential work by Xabier Itçaina (*Catholic Mediations in Southern Europe: The Invisible Politics of Religion*, London: Routledge 2018), as well as the excellent master's thesis by Jerémie Dedieu-Darquy, *La Nouvelle Évangélisation à l'épreuve du Pays basque. La communauté Saint-Martin dans le diocèse de Bayonne*, master's of contemporary history, University of Bordeaux-Montaigne, 2015.

20. Symbolic in this regard was the letter that John Paul II sent in February 2005, two months before his death, to the French episcopate for the anniversary of the Law of 1905 on the Separation of Church and State. In it he fully acknowledged the value of French secularity (*laïcité*), even if he encouraged

'cooperation' with this secularity, as was desired by the French episcopate.

21. After his death in 2008, it turned out that the Mexican priest Marcial Maciel Degollado, founder of the Legion of Christ in 1941, a congregation entirely devoted to the pope, had a number of secret lives: as a proven paedophile (abusing children and young legionnaires); a morphine addict; a swindler who led a life of luxury with several successive mistresses who bore him a number of children; and living with a young woman and a daughter he had by her. He escaped all internal accusations and enjoyed the protection of Pope John Paul II until the latter's death in 2005. Cardinal Ratzinger investigated the case in the early 2000s and in 2006, as Pope Benedict XVI, put an end to a most extraordinary career of depravity and perversion.

22. Let that be a warning to those who think Islam must be reformed before Muslims are allowed to participate in political life.

23. The Catholic Church has directed its lobbying efforts at European institutions via COMECE (the Commission of the Bishops' Conferences of the European Community) and the European Centre for Law and Justice, established in conjunction with American evangelicals.

24. Indifference to culture has become a permanent temptation among young Catholics influenced by intransigent charismatic movements. This was already very clear in the title of the book by Jean-Pierre Denis, editor-in-chief of the weekly *La Vie: Pourquoi le christianisme fait scandale. Éloge d'une contre-culture*, Paris: Seuil, 2010.

7. IDENTITY AND VALUES: EUROPE AND THE OTHER

1. James Davison Hunter, *Culture Wars*, New York: Basic Books, 1991.

2.   Samuel Huntington, *The Clash of Civilizations*, New York: Simon & Schuster, 1996.

3.   However, a trend among conservative Catholics would like to align the Church's 'social doctrine' with the economic ultraliberalism of Protestant evangelicals. Father Robert Sirico, whose personal trajectory is rather complex, has written in this vein in *Defending the Free Market: The Moral Case for a Free Economy*, Washington, DC: Regnery Publishing, 2012.

4.   In Europe, the Catholic Church defends Christians from the Middle East, who are mostly Arabs, while 'centrist' Protestants follow a line of defence of human rights and are therefore sensitive to the Palestinian cause. Relations between the Vatican and Israel are not particularly good.

5.   Front National poster during the 1978 election campaign.

6.   See Nadia Marzouki, Duncan McDonnell, Olivier Roy (eds), *Saving the People: How Populists Hijack Religion*, London: Hurst, 2016. The only exception is Poland's PiS, which campaigns for a Christian Poland and against Islam. The Fidesz in Hungary wields the rhetoric of Christian identity, but simply gives greater importance to churches without emphasizing a plan of (re)Christianization.

7.   The paganist movement is strong not only in the neo-Nazi far right in northern Europe, but also in the French far right. See Alain de Benoist: 'The more Christianity seeks to become "de-paganized", the less it resonates in the hearts of the masses who are especially sensitive to old popular traditions that have been sanctified over the centuries but that have actually existed since the dawn of time: processions, pilgrimages, celebrations that since prehistory have accompanied the rhythm of the seasons and the ages ... Catholicism is tied in with 2,000 years of European history. At the same time, it takes its source outside of Europe, in the prodigious destiny that the rich posterity of a little Jewish sect has experienced ... It is ... not forbidden, and even strongly advised, to resort to paganism

to find a dimension that fits into the long term, to better understand our origins', interview in *Terre et Peuple*, Lyon, September 2001.

8. *La Croix*, 4 May 2017.
9. There has always been an identitarian conservative Catholic current, from Action Française to the traditionalist wing of Front National (Bernard Antony's AGRIF, whose symbol is the cross borne by a Gallic cockerel). Today the 'Salon Beige' website represents this tendency by backing Marion Maréchal, but their intransigence means that they have remained on the fringes.
10. See below.
11. Lyon, 6 February 2007. Its signatories include the Catholic bishop, the chief rabbi, the imam of the Lyon mosque, Greek and Armenian Orthodox priests, as well as evangelical, Anglican and Lutheran ministers. Only the Reformed Church was absent, https://fr.zenit.org/articles/lyon-declaration-commune-de-chretiens-juifs-et-musulmans-sur-le-mariage
12. During a meeting in Trent in 2011 of Catholic diplomats and Tunisian members of the Nahda Party, Father Dall'Oglio (who has since disappeared in Syria) made a short but noted speech against this trend, arguing, with respect to same-sex marriage, to the effect that 'We are not legislators; we should be prophets.'
13. Rod Dreher, *The Benedict Option: A Strategy for Christians in a Post-Christian Nation*, New York: Sentinel, 2017. Like many conservative Catholics in the United States (Ross Douthat, Robert Sirico, Sam Brownback), Dreher was originally a Protestant before converting to Eastern Orthodoxy.
14. Interview in *Le Monde* on 11 January 2018 with Michel Aupetit, archbishop of Paris: 'The taboo today is no longer sex, it's God.'
15. Aupetit's statement is in entirely in line with Saint Augustine, who knew the meaning of decadence.
16. Montaigne, *Essais*, book II, chap. 12.

17. In its party programme for the 2017 presidential election, the Front National wanted to make secularism an essential principle of the Republic. ('Proposition 95: Promote secularism (*laïcité*) and combat communitarianism. Enshrine in the Constitution the following principle: "The Republic does not recognize any community." Re-establish secularism everywhere, extend it to the entire public sphere and enshrine it in the Labour Code.') Marine Le Pen makes secularism (laïcité) the weapon used to combat Islamism and mentions France's Christian heritage only in passing. She refuses to condemn abortion and same-sex marriage and invites Christians and Jews to reduce their own religious visibility as a means of reducing that of Islam (interview given in *Famille chrétienne*, 8 March 2017).

18. The Lega Nord newspaper wrote: 'Is he a bishop or an imam?' http://www.ilsole24ore.com/art/SoleOnLine4/Italia/2009/12/tettamanzi-polemiche-lega.shtml?uuid=641f6ebc-e324-11de-92fb-886fa561cf24&refresh_ce=1

19. *La Croix*, 19 October 2017.

20. Catholicism attaches a level of importance to images, sacred art and marking its territory, whereas Protestant intellectualism is reluctant to appeal to the senses.

21. Marine Le Pen's party platform for the 2012 presidential election. This clause no longer appeared in 2017.

22. 'Les vérités de Mgr Vingt-Trois', *Le Parisien*, 19 December 2017.

23. 'Kardinal Schönborn liest Strache die Leviten', *Die Presse*, 21 May 2009.

24. In June 2016, during a procession in San Paolo Bel Sito, near Naples, the bearers of the statue of the Madonna had her bow before the home of a local mafia boss. The bishop of Nola, Beniamino Depalma, had to intervene to defend the parish priest, who by that point had left the procession. Even Pope Francis got involved ('it is not the Virgin who bowed, it is only

astatue'),http://www.napolitoday.it/cronaca/inchino-madonna-san-paolo-belsito.html
25. Regarding the dancing procession in Echternach, Luxembourg, the archbishopric's newsletter wonders: 'Procession or Show? … In view of this evolution, organizers and participants should ask themselves whether the procession is not running a risk by becoming more colourful and spectacular. Is it in keeping with the nature of the procession to see each group try to make its origin visible in one way or another?' https://web.cathol.lu/2/mouvements/oeuvre-saint-willibrord/oeuvre-saint-willibrord/procession-dansante/le-sens-de-la-procession-dansante-d-echternach-et-sa-sauvegarde-precisions-utiles.html

8. THE END OF CHRISTIAN EUROPE OR THE END OF RELIGION?

1. Training courses in secularism for imams, organized by the Institut Catholique of Paris. Needless to say, there was a certain lack of conviction on both sides and the endeavour didn't last more than two years.
2. Olivier Roy, *Globalized Islam: The Search for a New Ummah*, London/New York: Hurst/Columbia University Press, 2004.
3. *L'Obs*, 22 January 2004.
4. See below.
5. Marianne Heimbach-Steins, 'Religious freedom and the German circumcision debate', EUI RSCAS, 2013/18, RELIGIOWEST, URI: http://hdl.handle.net/1814/26335
6. *La Croix*, 15 July 2012.
7. https://www.independent.co.uk/news/world/europe/denmark-bans-halal-and-kosher-slaughter-as-minister-says-animal-rights-come-before-religion-9135580.html
8. Genesis 1, 26 and 28.
9. Christopher Prowse, archbishop of Canberra and Goulburn, *Canberra Times*, 6 June 2018.

10. For the state of the discussion in France, see Francis Messner (ed.), *Traité de droit français des religions*, article 1416, Paris: Litec, 2003.

11. 'Manifeste contre le nouvel antisémitisme,' *Le Parisien*, 21 April 2018.

12. This has been to the great displeasure of Jean Marie Le Pen, who believes that hipsters are contributing to the tolerance of Islamism in France: https://www.youtube.com/watch?v=XqBMX2WfAtk

13. https://www.journaldesfemmes.com/maman/ado/1759910-radicalisation-terrorisme-prevention-adolescents

14. In fact, the UOIF (Union of Islamic Organizations in France) congresses at Le Bourget have witnessed the coming together of a new litany of Catholic saints: 'Islamic Association of Saint-Denis,' 'Islamic Association of Saint-Pierre,' 'Islamic Association of Saint-Hilaire-Saint-Mesmin,' etc.

15. To my knowledge, the proposal to include Jewish and Muslim holidays in the official calendar always comes from non-religious organizations, such as the Stasi Commission in 2004, and never from Muslim or Jewish religious communities, which have a sense of the sacred.

16. See Ruben Seth Fogel, 'Headscarves in German Public Schools,' *New York Law School Law Review*, vol. 51, no. 3, 2006–2007.

17. See Frederick Mark Gedicks and Pasquale Annicchino, 'Cross, Crucifix, Culture: An Approach to the Constitutional Meaning of Confessional Symbols,' EUI RSCAS, 2013/88; RELIGIOWEST, http://cadmus.eui.eu/handle/1814/29058

18. http://www.lastampa.it/2018/03/18/vaticaninsider/ita/vaticano/il-crocifisso-non-un-oggetto-ornamentale-o-un-accessorio-dabbigliamento-5OLAp7DthX6vBfZ0RHEXxL/pagina.html

19. See below.

20. The principle of subsidiarity is also present in the Christian tradition, found with the sixteenth-century Protestants as well

as in the encyclical *Rerum novarum* of 1891 and subsequent social encyclicals.

CONCLUSION

1. See a discussion of this principle in the famous dialogue between Jürgen Habermas and Joseph Ratzinger in 2004 at the Catholic Academy of Bavaria, in *Esprit*, July 2004, 'The Pre-Political Moral Foundations of a Liberal State', pp. 5–28 (published in book form as *The Dialectics of Secularization: On Reason and Religion*, trans. Brian McNeill, San Francisco, CA: Ignatius Press, 2007).

Index

abortion, 3, 6, 18, 47, 61, 63, 68, 81, 83, 84, 105, 110, 114, 118, 151
  in Brazil, 140
  in France, 3, 51, 76, 167*n*
  in Ireland, 31, 34
  as non-negotiable moral issue, 82, 99
  in United States, 84, 103–4
Action Française, 59
Ad tuendam fidem (1998), 158*n*
Adenauer, Konrad, 1
adoption, 78
adultery, 18, 47, 77
Æquum reputamus (1534), 21
Æterni Patris (1879), 48
aggiornamento, 40–41, 43, 64, 68, 69
AGRIF, 166*n*
Aillet, Marc, 91, 93
Alexander VII, Pope, 22
Alpha course, 90
al-Andalus (711–1492), 8

Anglicanism, 25, 28, 49, 85
anti-Semitism, 106
anticlericalism, 23, 30, 48, 49, 67, 116, 119, 158*n*
Antimodernist Oath (1910–67), 53
Antony, Bernard, 166*n*
Aquinas, Thomas, 94
Argentina, 95
artificial intelligence, 136
artificial procreation, 78, 99, 115
Attila the Hun, 117
Au milieu des sollicitudes (1892), 57
Augsburg Settlement (1555), 15
Augustine, Saint, 166*n*
Aupetit, Michel, 117–18, 166*n*
Australia, 139
Austria, 106, 108, 123, 149
awakening movements, 19, 60

Bagnasco, Angelo, 161*n*
BalanceTonPorc, 79
baptism, 2, 30, 87, 89, 97, 121, 138
Baptists, 62
Barbarians, 117
Barbarin, Philippe, 99, 108
Barmen Declaration (1934), 159*n*
Barth, Karl, 54, 159*n*
Basque Country, 93, 157*n*
Battle of the White Mountain (1620), 35
Bavaria, Germany, 86, 122, 128
de Beauvoir, Simone, 75–6
Belgium, 12, 28, 77, 108
Benedict Option (Dreher), 116, 166*n*
Benedict XIII, Pope, 49
Benedict XVI, Pope, 6, 59, 67, 96, 99–101
  and Degollado, 164*n*
  and deterritorialization, 96
  and European culture, 1, 3, 26, 111, 161*n*
  European Parliament address (2006), 82, 160*n*
  and laity, 91
  and liberation theology, 59
  non-negotiable moral issues, 82–3, 94, 97, 99, 101, 109, 112, 115, 138, 153
  and universalism, 96

de Benoist, Alain, 165*n*
Berlusconi, Silvio, 99
Bertolucci, Bernardo, 48
Biblical inerrancy, 52, 53
von Bismarck, Otto, 49
blasphemy, 18, 136–8, 149
Böckenförde, Ernst-Wolfgang, 152
Bohemia, 35
Bonhoeffer, Dietrich, 54, 60, 62, 159*n*
Boulard, Fernand, 38
Boutin, Christine, 79
Brague, Rémi, 6, 44, 90, 150
Brazil, 59, 93, 95, 140
Brittany, 34
Bruckner, Pascal, 5
burkinis, 142
burqa, 131, 148

Calvinism, 12, 13
Câmara, Hélder, 59, 95, 140
Canon Dangoisse,
capitalism, 13
Capture of Rome (1870), 23, 49
Cardonnel, Thomas, 59
Carron, Julian, 162*n*
cassocks, 85, 86, 129, 132
Casti connubii (1930), 81
Catholic Action, 58, 92, 94
Catholic Mothers Prayers, 90
Catholicism; Catholic Church
  Ad tuendam fidem (1998), 158*n*

Æquum *reputamus* (1534), 21

Æterni *Patris* (1879), 48

aggiornamento, 40–41, 43, 64, 68, 69

Antimodernist Oath (1910–67), 53

Au milieu des sollicitudes (1892), 57

Biblical inerrancy, 52, 53

Casti connubii (1930), 81

Catholic Action movement, 58, 92, 94

communion, 38, 65, 68, 84, 162*n*

confession, 10, 18, 38, 139–40

conversions, 30, 65, 159*n*

Council of Trent, 10, 12

dechristianization, 28–41

Eucharist, 64, 68, 69, 137, 139, 141

Evangelium vitæ (1995), 161

funeral masses, 29

Gaudium et Spes (1965), 66, 160*n*

Great Schism (1054), 9

Humanæ vitæ (1968), 2, 71, 81–2

inculturation, 24, 26, 59, 101

Inquisition, 5

Lamentabili sane exitu (1907), 53

Manif Pour Tous, La, 3, 5, 99

Maximam gravissimamque (1924), 158

Mirari Vos (1832), 52

missionaries, 21–6, 33

Mit Brennender Sorge (1937), 158

modernism and, 48–55, 57–8

mortmain properties, 48

Non expedit decree (1868), 19, 49

padroado, 21–2

Pascendi (1907), 52

Providentissimus Deus (1893), 53

Quanta cura (1864), 53

Rerum novarum (1891), 58

revivalism, 3, 24–5, 86–96, 163*n*

secularization, 27–41, 51, 54–5, 57–9, 63–9

supranationality, 10, 22–3

Syllabus Errorum (1864), 43, 53

Synod on the Family (2015–16), 84

Trinity, 68, 69

Vatican Council, First (1870), 23, 53

Vatican Council, Second (1962–5), 32–4, 36, 41, 43, 58–9, 63–9, 82, 87, 91, 108, 163*n*

Vehementer nos (1906), 53

celibacy, 65
Centro de Investigaciones Sociológicas, 38
charismatic movements, 24, 61, 87–96, 100
Charles V, Holy Roman Emperor, 15
Charles-de-Gaulle airport, Paris, 143
Charlie Hebdo, 5, 106
Chemin Neuf Community, 87
Childeric, King of the Franks, 117
Chile, 95
China, 22, 24, 61, 72, 142, 160*n*
Christian democracy, 50, 97–9, 116
Christian Democratic Union of Germany, 99
Christian Zionists, 104
Christin, Olivier, 14
Christmas, 4, 121–2
Chur, Switzerland, 95, 96
church attendance, 4, 29, 30, 35, 37, 38, 85, 86
circumcision, 6, 128, 131, 133–4
civil marriage, 47, 51
clash of civilizations, 103, 104–5, 106
Clovis I, King of the Franks, 2
Colbert, Jean-Baptiste, 21
Colloquy at Poissy (1561), 15
Colombia, 95

colonialism, 21–6
Combes, Émile, 68
Comité Laïcité République, 120
Commission of the Bishops' Conferences of the European Community, 164*n*
common law, 13
Communion and Liberation, 87, 91, 162*n*
communion, 38, 65, 68, 84, 162*n*
communism, 35, 47, 48, 147
Community of Saint-Martin, 87, 91, 93–4
Community of Sant'Egidio, 88, 90, 162*n*
Confessing Church, 13, 159*n*
confession, 10, 18, 38, 139
contraception, 51, 81, 82, 110
conversions, 30, 65, 159*n*
Council of Trent, 10, 12
Cox, Harvey, 63
Credo, 64
Crouzet, Denis, 14
crucifixes, 85–6, 122, 127, 128, 147–8
Cuchet, Guillaume, 32
cuisine, 12
Cultural Revolution (1966–76), 72, 160*n*
culture wars, 62, 103–9
Czech Republic, 35

Dall'Oglio, Paolo, 166*n*
De Gasperi, Alcide, 1
deacons, 90, 163*n*
dechristianization, 2, 18,
    27–41, 140
Declaration of the French
    Clergy (1682), 17
Dedieu-Darquy, Jérémie, 163*n*
Defending the Free Market
    (Sirico), 165*n*
Degollado, Marcial Maciel, 96,
    164*n*
Demonstration for All, 3, 5, 99
Denis, Jean-Pierre, 164*n*
Denmark, 37, 51, 107, 129,
    160*n*
Depalma, Beniamino, 167*n*
Descartes, René, 40, 44, 135
deterritorialization, 88, 96
Di Maio, Luigi, 99
Dies irae dies illa, 159*n*
Diet of Regensburg (1541–46),
    15
Diet of Worms (1557), 15
dissenting churches, 60
divorce, 31, 47, 68, 76, 129, 141
DNA (deoxyribonucleic acid),
    78
dominicantes, 35
Don Camillo films, 54
Dov̌e Dio? (Carron), 162*n*
Dreher, Ray Oliver 'Rod', 116,
    150, 166*n*

Easter, 4
Eastern Orthodox Church, 9
Echternach, Luxembourg,
    168*n*
Emmanuel Community, 87, 88
Enlightenment, 5, 74, 110
environmentalism, 74–5
Epistle to the Ephesians, 65
eruv, 153
ethology, 135–6
Eucharist, 64, 68, 69, 137, 139,
    141
European Court of Human
    Rights, 13, 127, 145, 147,
    148–50
European Economic
    Community (EEC), 1
European Parliament, 82, 160*n*
European Union, 73, 82
    constitution draft (2004), 1,
    2, 109
euthanasia, 99, 115
Evangelical Protestantism, 3,
    13, 84, 87, 90, 94, 103–5,
    165*n*

family, 10–11, 40, 47, 51
far right, 68, 86, 106–8, 120,
    165*n*
Fascism, 55
federalism, 20
female genital mutilation, 131
feminism, 75, 118, 119
Ferry, Jules, 40, 45–7, 72

Ferry, Luc, 132
fertility rates, 12
Feuerbach, Ludwig, 39
Fidesz, 165*n*
Fin des paysans, La (Mendras), 33
Finland, 51, 147
Florence, Italy, 113
Focolare Movement, 87, 90, 94
Forza Italia, 98
Foucault, Paul-Michel, 10
France, 2
   abortion in, 3, 51, 76
   Action Française, 59
   adultery in, 77
   AGRIF, 166*n*
   anticlericalism in, 23, 30, 49, 158*n*
   #BalanceTonPorc, 79
   blasphemy in, 137
   Chemin Neuf Community, 87
   Comité Laïcité République, 120
   communism in, 47–8
   Community of Saint-Martin, 87, 91, 93–4
   Declaration of the Clergy (1682), 17
   divorce in, 76
   Edict of Toleration for Protestants (1787), 17
   Emmanuel Community, 87, 88
   far right in, 4, 5, 38, 99, 106, 108, 110, 119, 120, 121, 165*n*
   Fight for the Larzac (1971–81), 73
   Front National, 4, 5, 38, 99, 106, 108, 110, 119, 121, 166*n*, 167*n*
   Gallicanism, 23, 27, 28
   headscarf controversies, 126, 132
   homosexuality in, 51
   identitarians in, 153–4
   laïcité, 4, 19, 28, 85, 109, 121–2, 130, 132, 142, 148, 155*n*, 163*n*, 167*n*
   Jules Ferry laws (1882), 45
   Law on the Separation of Church and State (1905), 19, 28, 45, 49, 53, 60, 68, 128, 142, 163*n*
   Manif Pour Tous, La, 3, 5, 99
   May 1968 protests, 72
   Mission Évangélique des Tziganes, 61
   National Bloc, 51
   nativity scenes in, 121–2
   New France (1534–1763), 21
   Notre-Dame-des-Landes airport, 73
   nuclear family in, 40
   Penal Code (1810), 51

prisons in, 142–3

Republic, papal recognition of (1890), 57

Revolution (1789–99), 18, 44, 75, 156n

Riposte laïque, 120

secularization, 30–31, 32, 37, 40, 45–8

Sillon movement, 158n

Society of Saint Pius X, 67–8

ultramontanism, 23

Veilleurs, Les, 99

Wars of Religion (c. 1532–1648), 14–15

France, pays de mission? (Godin), 33

Francis, Pope, 5, 25, 26, 67, 68, 83–4, 100, 106, 109

Franco, Francisco, 50

François I, King of France, 15

Freedom Party of Austria, 123

Freiheitliche Partei Österreichs (FPÖ), 123

Front National, 4, 5, 38, 99, 106, 108, 110, 119, 121, 166n, 167n

fundamentalism, 61, 91

funerals, 29, 159n

Gallicanism, 23, 27, 28

Gauchet, Marcel, 39, 44, 158n

Gaudium et Spes (1965), 66, 160n

de Gaulle, Charles, 28

gay marriage, *see* same-sex marriage

gender fluidity, 75–6

gender, 29, 110

Geneviève, Saint, 117

Germany, 4, 28

Barmen Declaration (1934), 159n

Catholic Centre Party, 50

Christian democracy in, 98, 99

circumcision in, 133–4

Confessing Church, 13

crucifix law (2018), 86, 122, 128

far right in, 106

homosexuality in, 51

Kulturkampf (1871–8), 49, 51, 60

Leitkultur, 128, 132, 148

Lutheran Church, 54, 60

Nazi period (1933–45), 13, 54, 55, 60, 62, 158n, 159n

populism, 107

refugee crisis (2015–16), 99

statutory corporations, 129–30

Stuttgart urban development project, 73

Giro, Mario, 162n

Giscard d'Estaing, Valéry, 76

Global South, 24–5, 61

Godin, Henri, 33

Good Friday Agreement (1998), 34
Good Friday prayer, 65, 159*n*
Grab, Amédée, 95
Gramsci, Antonio, 54
Great Schism (1054), 9
Gregory IX, Pope, 9
Gregory XVI, Pope, 52
Guardian, The, 78
Guareschi, Giovannino, 54
Gutiérrez, Gustavo, 59
Gypsy Evangelical Mission, 61

Haas, Wolfgang, 95, 96
Habermas, Jürgen, 66
Habsburg Monarchy, 27, 35
halakha, 141
Hamel, Jacques, 161*n*
Hamilton, David, 160*n*
von Harnack, Adolf, 62
headscarves, 126, 131–2, 145–6
Hegel, Georg Wilhelm Friedrich, 39
Henri IV, King of France, 30
hijab, 126, 131–2
Holy Roman Empire, 15–16
homosexuality, 5, 25, 47, 51, 84, 94, 106, 110, 119
  same-sex marriage, *see* same-sex marriage
hotel rooms, 12
Humanæ vitæ (1968), 2, 71, 81–2
Hungary, 165*n*

Hunter, James Davison, 103
Huntington, Samuel, 103, 104–5, 106

identitarians, 39, 108, 125, 145, 150, 151, 153–4, 166*n*
identity, 1, 4–6, 36–41, 61–2, 68, 84, 101, 103–12, 118–24, 153
immigration, 2, 3, 61, 73, 103, 104–5, 106, 109, 110
inculturation, 24, 26, 59, 101
indigenization, 59
Inquisition, 5
Iran, 20, 68, 126
Ireland, 12, 31, 33–4, 35, 76–7, 115
Islam, 3, 4, 5, 6, 13, 39, 112–14, 125–50
  alcohol, 143
  blasphemy and, 136, 149
  Christian identity and, 4, 5, 39, 68, 86, 104–5, 109, 121, 123, 125–31
  circumcision, 6, 128, 131, 133–4
  conversion from, 30
  family values, 85
  headscarves, 126, 131–2, 145–6
  immigration and, 2, 4, 104–5, 106, 109, 110–11, 112, 117, 120
  interfaith dialogue, 91, 112

minarets, 13, 128, 146–7
mosques, 113, 121, 146–7
populism and, 2, 104–5, 106, 107, 109, 110, 118, 120
Qur'an, 21, 130, 131, 141, 142
ritual slaughter, 6, 131, 134, 135
Salafism, 125, 143
and same-sex marriage, 113
secularism and, 5, 15, 106, 110–11, 125
states, relations with, 20–21
Islamic State, 126
Israel, 165n
Italy
  Christian Democracy, 50, 98
  Communion and Liberation, 87, 91, 162n
  Community of Sant'Egidio, 88, 90, 162n
  crucifixes in, 127, 147–8
  divorce in, 76
  far right in, 106
  Fascist period (1922–43), 55
  Focolare Movement, 87, 90, 94
  Forza Italia, 98
  homosexuality in, 51
  Italian People's Party, 50
  Lega Nord, 107, 120
  mafia, 167n
  NO TAV movement (1995–), 73

Non expedit decree (1868), 19, 49
  populism in, 99, 106, 119, 120
  unification (1815–71), 19, 28, 49
Itçaina, Xabier, 157n, 163n

Janatha Vimukthi Peramuna insurrection (1987–9), 72
Japan, 72
Jesuits, 22, 24, 49
Jesus, 37, 64, 137–8
John Paul II, Pope, 2–3, 35, 67, 96, 99–100, 104, 110, 140
  Ad tuendam fidem (1998), 158n
  and baptism, 2–3
  and celibacy, 65
  and charismatic networks, 94–5
  and Degollado, 164n
  and deterritorialization, 96
  and European culture, 26, 111
  Evangelium vitæ (1995), 161
  and laity, 91, 92
  laïcité, acknowledgement of (2005), 163–4n
  and liberation theology, 59
  and paedophilia, 67
  and universalism, 96
  and US conservatives, 104

John XXIII, Pope, 67
Jorgensen, Dan, 135
Josephinism, 27
Judaism, 6, 8–9, 65, 67, 113, 129, 132, 134, 153, 159*n*

Kant, Immanuel, 44
Kenya, 25
Kir, Félix, 129
Kulturkampf (1871–8), 49, 51, 60

Lacan, Jacques, 10
laïcité, 4, 19, 28, 85, 109, 121–2, 130, 132, 142, 148, 155*n*, 163*n*, 167*n*
laity, 50, 87–96, 162*n*
Lamentabili sane exitu (1907), 53
Landsknechte, 16
Last Supper, The (Leonardo da Vinci), 137
Lavigerie, Charles, 57
Law and Justice, 36, 110, 119
Le Bras, Gabriel, 38
Le Cossec, Pastor, 61
Le Pen, Jean-Marie, 5, 38
Le Pen, Marine, 99, 110, 119, 121, 167*n*
Lefebvre, Marcel, 67, 162*n*
Lega Nord, 107, 120
Legendre, Pierre, 39
Legion of Christ, 96, 164*n*
Legutko, Ryszard, 6

Leitkultur, 128, 132, 148
Leo XIII, Pope, 48, 53, 57
Leonardo da Vinci, 137
liberalism, 25, 50, 52, 60, 62, 103–7, 109, 111, 152–3
liberation theology, 59
Libération, 160*n*
libertarianism, 73, 74, 78
Loisy, Alfred, 53
López Trujillo, Alfonso, 95
Louis XIV, King of France, 17, 28
Lubich, Chiara, 94
Ludin, Fereshta, 145
Lustiger, Jean-Marie, 95
Luther, Martin, 11, 14, 15, 71, 156*n*
Lutheranism, 12, 13, 16, 17, 35, 36, 60, 85, 107
Luxembourg, 168*n*

Macron, Emmanuel, 69
mafia, 123, 167*n*
Magdalene laundries, 34
Malle, Louis, 160*n*
Manent, Pierre, 6, 150
Manif Pour Tous, La, 3, 5, 99
Maréchal, Marion, 99, 110, 166*n*
Marithé et François Girbaud, 137
marriage, 30, 82, 89
    adultery, 18, 47, 77
    civil marriage, 47, 51

divorce, 31, 47, 68, 76, 84, 129, 141
Epistle to the Ephesians, 65
obedience and, 65, 77
polygamy, 136
same-sex marriage, *see* same-sex marriage
Marx, Reinhard, 122
Marxism, 72
Mary, Mother of Jesus, 37, 69, 123
mass, 4, 29, 30, 35, 37, 38, 86–7, 89
masturbation, 140
Maurras, Charles, 38
Maximam gravissimamque (1924), 158
Meisner, Joachim, 134
Mendras, Henri, 33
Merkel, Angela, 99
MeToo movement, 74, 79, 119
Mexico, 22, 72, 96, 164*n*
millenarianism, 66
minarets, 13, 128, 146–7
Mirari Vos (1832), 52
Mission Évangélique des Tziganes de France, 61
missionaries, 21–6, 33, 61
Mit Brennender Sorge (1937), 158
Mitterrand, François, 69
modernism, 48–55, 57–8, 67, 80, 97
Mohammed bin Salman, 156*n*

Monde, Le, 117, 160*n*, 161*n*
Mondo Piccolo stories (Guareschi), 54
de Montaigne, Michel, 118
mortmain properties, 48
mosques, 113, 121, 146–7
Muhammad, Prophet of Islam, 138, 146, 149
Muslim Brotherhood, 126

Nahda Party, 166*n*
National Bloc, 51
nationalism, 31, 34–6, 157*n*
nativity scenes, 121–2
natural law, 10, 48, 51, 52, 83, 94, 97, 100, 111
Nazi Germany (1933–45), 13, 54, 55, 60, 62, 158*n*, 159*n*
neo-Nazism, 104, 165*n*
neoliberalism, 73
Netherlands, 12, 51, 60, 77, 106, 107, 110, 119
Nigeria, 25
NO TAV movement (1995–), 73
Non expedit decree (1868), 19, 49
non-negotiable moral issues, 82, 94, 97, 99, 101, 109, 112, 115, 138, 153
Northern Ireland, 34, 36
Norway, 51, 60, 107
nuclear family, 10–11, 40, 47, 51

Oasis International Foundation, 91
L'Obs, 78
Opus Dei, 95
organic food, 74

paedophilia, 34, 74, 79, 115, 116, 139, 149, 163*n*, 164*n*
paganism, 2–3, 83, 88, 107, 108, 116, 117, 161*n*, 165*n*
Palestine, 165*n*
Papal Zouaves, 23
Paraguay, 22
parental leave, 77
parenthood, 77–8, 160*n*
Partido Popular, 98
Pascal, Blaise, 136, 150
Pascendi (1907), 52
Pastoral Constitution (1965), 66, 160*n*
Paul III, Pope, 21, 22
Paul VI, Pope, 2, 71
Peace of Augsburg (1555), 15
Peace of Westphalia (1648), 11, 13–14, 16, 27, 67, 130, 149
Pegida, 107
Pentecost, 4
Pentecostalism, 61
Pera, Marcello, 6
Peru, 95
Petite, *La*, 160*n*
Pierre, Abbé, 85, 129
PiS (Prawo i Sprawiedliwość), 36, 110, 119, 165*n*

Pius IX, Pope, 52, 53, 57
Pius X, Pope, 49, 52, 53, 57
Pius XI, Pope, 81, 158*n*
Pius XII, Pope, 59, 158*n*
Polak, Wojciech, 120
Poland, 35, 36, 110, 115, 119
polygamy, 136
populism, 2, 4, 13, 39, 73, 84, 99, 101, 105–11, 114, 116, 118–24, 153
Portugal, 21, 22, 108
processions, 94, 123, 128, 165*n*, 167–8*n*
procreation, 54, 66, 71, 75, 77–8, 82–3, 99, 115, 151
prostitution, 18
Protestantism, 3, 11–14, 60–63, 163*n*
   awakening movements, 19, 60
   in Bohemia, 35
   Calvinism, 12
   dechristianization, 32, 37
   Evangelicalism, 3, 13, 84, 87, 90, 94, 103–5, 107, 165*n*
   fundamentalism, 61
   liberalism, 25, 60, 62
   Lutheranism, 12, 13, 16, 17, 35, 36, 85, 107
   Pentecostalism, 61
   Reformation, 11–12, 14, 16
   revivalism, 3, 24–5, 61, 87
   secularization, 60–63, 67, 85

state, relations with, 54
and values, 107
in United States, 12, 13
Providentissimus Deus (1893),
53
Prowse, Christopher, 139
psychoanalysis, 10

al-Qaeda, 126
Quanta cura (1864), 53
Quebec, Canada, 32, 34, 35
Qur'an, 21, 130, 131, 141, 142

rape, 136, 140
Ratzinger, Joseph, *see* Benedict
XVI
Reagan, Ronald, 104
reasonable accommodation,
153
Recife, Brazil, 59, 95, 140
Reformation, 11–12, 14, 16
refugees, 99, 112, 120
relativism, 50, 52, 83, 114
Renzi, Matteo, 98
reproduction, *see* procreation
Rerum novarum (1891), 58
revivalism
Catholic, 3, 24–5, 86–96,
163*n*
Protestant, 3, 24–5, 61, 87
Rey, Dominique, 91
Riposte laïque, 120
ritual slaughter, 6, 131, 134,
135–6

Rivera y Damas, Arturo, 95
Robespierre, Maximilien, 18,
156*n*
Rod Dreher,
Roma, 120
Roman Empire, 116–18
Roman law, 11, 13
Rome
capture of (1870), 23, 49
sack of (1527), 16
Romero y Galdámez, Óscar
Arnulfo, 95
Rushdie, Salman, 136
Russian Orthodox Church, 35

Sack of Rome (1527), 16
Sacred Congregation for the
Propagation of the Faith, 22
Saint-Nicolas-du-Chardonnet
Church, Paris, 68
Salafism, 125, 143
Salon Beige, 166*n*
Salvini, Matteo, 99, 106, 119,
120
same-sex marriage, 3, 6, 77,
79, 105, 107, 108, 114, 151,
166*n*
in Belgium, 77
in France, 3, 99, 167*n*
in Ireland, 31
Lyon declaration (2007), 113
in Netherlands, 77
as non-negotiable moral
issue, 94, 99

populists and, 118
Protestantism and, 61, 63
in Spain, 77
in United States, 103–4, 139
San Salvador, 95
Sangnier, Marc, 158n
Sarah, Robert, 25
Sartre, Jean-Paul, 64
Satanic Verses, The (Rushdie),
136
Satanism, 83
Saudi Arabia, 20, 142, 156n
Savonarola, Girolamo, 20
Schlegel, Jean-Louis, 163n
Schleiermacher, Friedrich, 60,
62
Schönborn, Christoph, 123
Schuman, Robert, 1
Scola, Angelo, 91
Secular City, The (Cox), 63
secularization, 27–41, 51,
54–5, 85, 114, 115, 131–50
self-secularization, 57–69,
85, 92, 115
Seehofer, Horst, 4
self-secularization, 57–69, 85,
92, 115
Sens Commun, 3
sex; sexuality, 2, 5, 66, 71,
81–2, 100, 110, 161n
adultery, 18, 47, 77
contraception, 51, 81, 82, 110
freedom, 2, 5, 48, 81, 110,
118

gender fluidity, 75–6
homosexuality, *see*
homosexuality
hotel rooms and, 12
Humanæ vitæ (1968), 2, 71,
81–2
#MeToo movement, 74, 79,
119
paedophilia, 34, 74, 79, 115,
116, 139, 163n, 164n
procreation, 54, 66, 71, 75,
77–8, 82–3, 99, 115, 151
prostitution, 18
Sixties culture and, 73, 74
transgenderism, 75
Shrove Tuesday, 5
Sikhism, 132
Sillon movement, 158n
sin, 18, 47, 79, 139–40
Sirico, Robert, 165n
Sixties culture, 71–80, 83, 110,
114, 119, 138
Sobrinho, José Cardoso, 95,
140
social contract theory, 152–3
social democracy, 61
socialism, 58, 60
Society of Foreign Missions,
22
Society of Jesus, 22, 24, 49
Society of Saint Pius X, 67–8,
162n
Sonderbund War (1847), 48–9,
60

South Korea, 25
Spain, 21, 31, 38, 48, 50, 77, 98, 108
Sri Lanka, 72
Stuttgart, Germany, 73, 145
Süddeutsche Zeitung, 122
suicide rates, 12, 83
supranationality, 10
Sweden, 106
Switzerland, 13, 23, 48, 60, 95, 107, 128, 132
Syllabus Errorum (1864), 43, 53
symbols, 85–6, 120–24, 126–32, 142, 144
Synod on the Family (2015–16), 84, 160*n*

Talmud, 9
Tamils, 61
Taylor, Charles, 153
Tettamanzi, Dionigi, 120
Thomism, 48
trade unions, 60
tradismatic movements, 87–96
transgenderism, 75
transubstantiation, 68
Travellers, 61
Treaty of Rome (1957), 1
Treaty of Westphalia (1648), 11, 13–14, 16, 27, 67, 130, 149
Trinity, 68, 69
Trump, Donald, 104

Tunisia, 166*n*
Turkey, 2

Uganda, 25
ultramontanism, 23
United Kingdom, 36
    blasphemy in, 136
    Church of England, 28, 49, 129
    cuisine, 12
    homosexuality in, 51
    Labour Party, 60
    Northern Ireland, 34, 36
    populism, 107
    Roman Catholic Relief Act (1829), 17
United States, 12, 13, 17, 19, 25, 28
    Americanist Catholicism, 49
    awakening movements, 19
    Baptists, 62
    culture wars, 62, 103–5
    Evangelical Protestantism, 3, 13, 84, 87, 94, 103–5, 107
    First Amendment (1791), 17, 19
    immigration in, 103–5, 107
    missionaries, 25
    Protestantism, 3, 12, 13, 84, 87, 94, 103–5
    same-sex marriage in, 103–4, 139

separation of church and state, 19, 28
universalism, 96, 100, 101, 108
University of Leuven, 108

values, 103–12, 119, 122, 125, 136, 141, 146, 151–4
Vatican Council
   First (1870), 23, 53
   Second (1962–5), 32–4, 36, 41, 43, 58–9, 63–9, 82, 87, 91, 108, 163*n*
vegetarianism, 74
Vehementer nos (1906), 53
Veilleurs, Les, 99
Vermeersch, Jeannette, 48
Vie, La, 164

Vingt-Trois, André, 95, 121, 161*n*

Wars of Religion (1517–1648), 14–15, 18
Weber, Maximilian, 13, 39
welfare state, 107
Westphalia, treaties of (1648), 11, 13–14, 16, 27, 67, 130, 149
Wilders, Geert, 106, 110, 119
women; women's rights, 29, 47, 75–6, 82, 163*n*
World Youth Days, 95, 161*n*

Zengakuren, 72
Zionism, 104